DRIVEN
NO MORE

*Finding Contentment
by Letting Go*

SCOTT WALKER

Augsburg
MINNEAPOLIS

DRIVEN NO MORE
Finding Contentment by Letting Go

Scripture passages are from the New American Standard Bible, copyright © 1960, 1962, 1963, 1968, 1971, 1972, 1973, 1975, 1977 The Lockman Foundation. Used by permission.

Cover image copyright © 2001 PhotoDisc. Used by permission.
Cover design by Timothy W. Larson
Book design by Timothy W. Larson and Michelle L. Norstad

Library of Congress Cataloging-in-Publication Data

Walker, Scott, –
   Driven no more: finding contentment by letting go / Scott Walker.
      p.cm.
   Includes bibliographical references.
   ISBN 0-8066-4251-3 (alk. paper)
   1. Contentment—Religious aspects—Christianity. 2. Self-actualization (Psychology)—Religious aspects—Christianity. 3. Compulsive behavior—Religious aspects—Christianity. 4. Christian life—Baptist authors. I. Title.

BV4647.C7 W35 2001
248.4—dc21   00-050221

The paper used in this publication meets the minimum requirements of American National Standard for Information Sciences—Permanence of Paper for Printed Library Materials, ANSI Z329.48-1984.

Manufactured in the U.S.A.   AF 9-4251

05   04   03   02   01   1   2   3   4   5   6   7   8   9   10

DRIVEN
NO MORE

To Bryant and Peggy Hicks,
whose love and enduring friendship
have brought me to freedom and safe harbor

CONTENTS

ACKNOWLEDGMENTS

I WOULD LIKE TO EXPRESS my deepest appreciation to the following people:

To Floyd Thatcher for his personal encouragement, friendship, direction, and literary guidance throughout the years;

To John and Beverly Bradley for the gracious use of their beach house in which to write;

To Martha Rosenquist, my editor, for her personal interest in this book and the excellent editorial direction;

And most of all, to my family—Beth, Drew, Luke, and Jodi—for their love, support, and selfless understanding.

Most of the stories in this book are "composite pictures"—bits and pieces of many lives pieced together to form a story that did not happen to one specific person. Names, locations, sex, and descriptions have been changed to protect the identities of people referred to in this book. When true names or stories have been related, written permission has been granted.

Introduction

HOW CAN WE
STOP BEING DRIVEN?

I N THE LATE EIGHTEENTH CENTURY, Samuel Taylor Coleridge wrote a story in verse titled "The Rime of the Ancient Mariner." In this tale he muses on the nature of the ocean, of life, and of death. In one memorable scene a man who is suffering from thirst looks at the vast ocean and with parched lips proclaims, "Water, water, everywhere, nor any drop to drink."[1]

I have thought of this poetic line many times as I have listened to the life stories of my neighbors, friends, and parishioners—"Water, water, everywhere, nor any drop to drink." The irony of American life is that we are surrounded by a vast freshwater ocean of things to enjoy and relish, yet we have a hard time giving ourselves the freedom to partake of it.

Our forefathers fought desperately for what we have inherited. They fought the British Empire for the freedom of self-government and the ideals of democracy. They fought the hostile elements of a "New World" to build an economy and a standard of living unrivaled in world history. They had a dream for their descendants. And that dream was for their sons and daughters to live in prosperity and freedom—to enjoy fully the good things of life.

1

However, as I look around me today, I repeatedly hear the haunting echo of Coleridge's mariner, "Water, water, everywhere, nor any drop to drink." We are surrounded by oceans of affluence, possessions, recreation, leisure, knowledge, and beauty. Yet, somehow, many are dying of thirst. Something is keeping them from drinking deeply of the fullness of life. Irony of ironies, in "the land of the free," many people are bound and imprisoned. They are enslaved by harmful internal forces driving them toward destruction. Sadly, they cannot let go of their own personal "drivenness" and find contentment and inner peace.

The tragic malady affecting so many of us today is our inability to find a sense of internal freedom and equilibrium that will permit us to slow down, relax, be ourselves, and enjoy life. Instead we are pushed and pulled by a thousand colliding forces. We are goaded by work and fame and the lure of possessions. We are agitated by insecurity, secrecy, and shame. We are hounded by wrenching feelings of loneliness, emptiness, and doubt. And this internal drivenness keeps us living on the edge because the center of life is completely out of control.

Our forefathers fought the tangible, external frontiers, but the greatest frontier is yet to be conquered: the emotional and spiritual frontier within us. We've had the imagination to develop and guide space vehicles to the outer limits of the known universe. And we're able to use the laser beam in delicate surgery. But for all of our technological advances, so many of us continue to be enslaved by the tyranny of unbridled drivenness.

As I ponder my own need to be driven no more, my mind drifts back across the years to two scenes. The first occurred when I was five years old. It was a hot summer night in South Carolina. I was excited and fully alive, for it was the grand occasion of witnessing my first "picture show."

Looking from our 1949 Hudson and sitting on a plump pillow between my parents, I found the drive-in theater a place of animated wonder. As twilight turned to darkness, Momma told me we were going to see a movie about a great, white whale named Moby Dick. As I listened to the crackling dialogue over the tinny window speakers, I was enamored with the story. I remember vividly the thrill of seeing the mammoth whale surging up from the deep and splintering whaling boats into kindling. That night the magic of the name *Moby Dick* gained a foothold in the deep recesses of my childhood memory.

The second related scene occurred in my senior year at college when my literature professor breathed life for me into the other great character in Herman Melville's *Moby Dick:* Captain Ahab. When I was five, my attention had been absorbed by the antics of the huge white whale. I had missed completely the penetrating complexity of Captain Ahab. But when I was a college senior, the story came together with a shattering force.

Ahab was a sea captain, a respected and industrious whaler, who had suffered a tragic humiliation and injury. Ahab's life had been blighted when a huge albino whale, Moby Dick, smashed against his boat, shattering the hull, and bit off a portion of Ahab's leg. From that day on Ahab had never been the same.

Embittered by the loss of his leg, Ahab crossed the fine line from being industrious and free to becoming enslaved and driven. Limping on his peg leg, he was driven by the crippling obsession to get revenge and could think of nothing else in his relentless search for Moby Dick. He was compelled—obsessively compelled—to destroy the whale, the source of his pain.

As I have looked into my own soul and have observed the lives of those I know well, I have come to see that the specter of Ahab casts a shadow over many of us. Somewhere in life we, too, have been wounded. And now the pain of our woundedness is pressing us to perform, to labor, to achieve, to prove ourselves, to self-destruct, to do whatever it takes to kill or numb the source of our unresolved pain. To be hounded and spurred through life, to be driven, seems to be a common malady. And so we must ask, "What exactly is this 'drivenness'?"

Scooting around house,
Dancing with Lois
Date with Jane
OSU - MICH, 1968, Press Box

A DEFINITION OF DRIVENNESS

What does it mean to be driven? And what differentiates a driven person from a free person who has a healthy sense of ambition, aspiration, and the energy to accomplish things in life?

I think that perhaps the primary difference is in the identity of who is sitting in the "driver's seat" of your life. Are you giving direction to your life? Or is somebody or something pushing, pressing, or directing you?

Healthy, ambitious people exhibit a full charge of energy and industry. Normally this energy is channeled toward achieving personally selected goals or objectives. Ambitious people have a high sense of self-motivation and self-direction. They eagerly engage life and find fulfillment in the journey.

Most important, healthy ambitious people are directed by a sense of fulfilling their own life's dream. That is, although we are influenced by and encouraged by other people, we move on our own toward goals and objectives that are self-selected and congenial with our self-identity. As healthy ambitious people we are not being robbed of our freedom by a taskmaster (real or internalized) or by an overbearing parent (dead or alive) or by a sense of guilt (deserved or undeserved) or by an agenda that is not our own.

Conversely, driven people may seem to give every appearance of being normally ambitious and full of commitment and energy, yet there are important and subtle differences. Driven people are not acting out of a true sense of self-fulfillment. People who are driven don't call their own shots. Indeed, to be driven, according to my dictionary, is "to be sent in some direction by blows, threats, violence . . . to be compelled, to overwork."[2] This simply means that driven people are being forced through life by "blows, threats, violence" in the past that are pushing them toward achievement or destruction. Driven people are "compelled and overworked"—out of control and enslaved to forces and motivations they do not understand. Freedom to live a rich and full life has given way to a slavish drivenness. Such people have no freedom.

In a rare moment of introspection, Captain Ahab recognized his own plight. Muttering to himself in the silence of the night, he exclaimed bitterly, "What is it, what nameless, inscrutable, unearthly thing is it . . . I so keep pushing and crowding, and jamming myself on all the time?"[3] Ahab knew that deep in his soul, some "nameless, inscrutable" thing was driving him along in life and robbing him of peace. His bitterness over what had happened to him had made him unhealthy and unstable.

THE RESULT OF DRIVENNESS

The end result of a driven life left unexamined and out of control is usually self-destruction. When Ahab finally found Moby Dick and plunged his harpoon deep into the whale's side, it cost him and his crew their lives.

So many contemporary Americans are paying a high price for their out-of-control drivenness. For instance, I know a man in his forties who has slaved for years to achieve financial security, yet now that he has it he continues to put in fourteen- and sixteen-hour work days. On Saturday he is unable to relax, and he seldom takes vacations. But the greatest tragedy is that he is a stranger in his own home.

My friend is rushing pell-mell toward self-destruction. And, in his compulsion to achieve, he cannot enjoy the life he has fashioned for himself. In addition, he is eroding his relationship with his wife and his children.

Yet he refuses to examine his motivation or change his ways. Late at night, in exhausted reflection, he will admit that he is pushed and shoved by forces he does not understand. But the next morning he is back into the same routine again. In attempting to numb his pain he eats too much, drinks too much, and pops an assortment of pills. He is wildly out of control.

As a result, he is a candidate for a heart attack, has lost contact with his children, and intimacy has disappeared from his marriage. Even though he is the epitome of success and is admired by his peers, he knows that the cruelest of all ironies is that he cannot give himself permission to enjoy and savor the fruit of his labor.

Does this sound extreme? It's not. Many of us walk a tightrope between healthy ambition and destructive drivenness. We vacillate from day to day as to who and what is in control of our lives. We desperately need to call a truce and explore the source of our compelling pain and the root of our destruction. In short, we need to be driven no more.

LEARNING TO LET GO

Socrates said centuries ago that "the unexamined life is not worth living." This phrase has become a classic statement of wisdom, and generations of people have recognized its authentic ring of truth. Not to examine our lives, our goals, and our motivation is to create a life for ourselves that is not worth living. It is to invite the destructive power of drivenness to overwhelm us.

In order to reduce the strength of unhealthy compulsive behavior in our lives, we must first look within ourselves and discover what it is that is so relentlessly pushing and pulling us. To explore the darkness of our lives is always a little scary. But it is a prerequisite for gaining control and finding a cure for our drivenness.

As we examine together those forces that can move us from being healthy and free to becoming victims of compulsive drivenness, we will see that it is the unhealed wounds of our life—wounds that fester and don't go away—that spark and stoke the fire of our restlessness.

All of us, to varying degrees, have been in some way injured by life. From the moment our umbilical cord was traumatically severed at birth, we have been vulnerable to the injuries of life. Later, as children, we may have encountered additional wounds from not receiving all the love we needed, or the attention we craved, or the understanding we sought, or the discipline we required.

Then, in the tumult of teenage years, we inevitably encountered the wrenching emotion of guilt and insecurity as the innocence of childhood was snatched away. We wrestled with self-doubt and awkwardness. And we soon discovered that to grow is to be wounded and that to mature is to know pain.

Now, as adults, we must recognize and come to terms with our woundedness. By doing so, we can be released—freed—from our drivenness. But first we must confront boldly the rain of unresolved emotional injuries; and, unlike Captain Ahab, we must identify that "nameless, inscrutable, unearthly" pain that is driving us toward emotional and spiritual destruction. Then, and only then, can we move toward healing and find contentment and peace.

Chapter One

ACCEPT
THE BLESSING

S USAN AND I HAD BEEN in a counseling relationship for several
weeks. At first words had come slowly. There was a fragile timidity in the air. But now her self-assured veneer was being slowly
stripped away, and the grain of her true self was beginning to appear.

On the day we met I was struck by her physical beauty. Tall,
shapely, with long brown hair, she had eyes that were captivating. Yet
I quickly saw that her intelligence and highly developed intellect
outshone her physical attraction. A lawyer, she could analyze a complex situation with ease and present her case with convincing credi-
bility. She had a warm personality, but at the same time she exuded
a professionalism. She elicited respect and was clearly on her way up.

As we talked, however, it soon became clear that though she
could convince a jury with ease, the one person she could not get to
vote for her was herself. She was filled with self-doubt and a feeling
of confidence-sapping unworthiness.

It was hard to believe this beautiful and talented woman, who
had so much going for her, saw herself as a mere survivor, a "plain
Jane" with limited gifts and glaring faults. And yet, because I have had
many similar conversations with numerous other people, I could
believe it. So many attractive and gifted people, both men and
women, see themselves as "bad" and "worthless." Over and over, the

universal fairy-tale theme of the prince or princess being turned into a frog is reenacted. And people of incalculable worth, beauty, and ability choose to live out the playwright's script that says they are frogs.

Low self-esteem is the number one malady of Americans. In a literate and success-oriented society where many people have so much, these same people look within themselves and see so little. Why?

This problem has many interrelated causes. But by far the greatest single contributor to a poor self-image and a lack of self-esteem is, in my opinion, a dynamic that is often called "the blessing." What is the blessing?

THE BLESSING

American and Western thought has been greatly influenced by Judeo-Christian concepts. The term *the blessing* comes from our Jewish heritage.

The Hebrew root word we translate as "blessing" literally means "to speak well of" or "to praise." The opposite of "to bless" is "to curse."

In the strongly paternalistic ancient Hebrew society, it was the duty of the father to give his sons—particularly the eldest—his blessing. Often this blessing was given near the time of the father's death as an act of bestowing inheritance. This form of the blessing is poignantly pictured in the book of Genesis, when blind and ailing Isaac calls his oldest son Esau to kneel before him so that he might place his hands ceremoniously upon his head and give his son the blessing. But Jacob, the younger son, tricked his father and older brother. He knelt before the blind old man, disguised as Esau, and Isaac unwittingly gave Jacob the paternal blessing (Gen. 27:1-40).

The blessing meant far more, however, than just receiving inheritance and possessions. It also spoke of the father's love, acceptance, and praise of the son. It signified that the father "spoke well" of his child. Symbolically it said to the young man, "You are pleasing to me. You are worthy of my trust, my lineage, my love, the profit of my lifetime. I am proud of you."

Most significant, the blessing—though accumulated over the course of years—could come to a boy only from his father and was for all time. Whether or not a Hebrew son received his father's blessing had a tremendous impact on his future. As an ancient Jewish maxim states, "The blessing of the father builds the children's house."[1]

Today the term *the blessing* is used to describe a very important emotional and psychological dynamic that transpires between parents and their children.[2] This dynamic centers on whether or not children grow up feeling that their parents—both father and mother—"speak well of them" or "praise them" and, in short, give them their blessing. Though this sense of blessing is not given in an official ceremony, as in ancient times, it is nonetheless meted out verbally and nonverbally throughout childhood and adolescence. By the time teenagers leave home to face their own uncertain future, they intuitively know whether or not they have received the blessing, or even a partial blessing.

When children are fortunate enough to enter adulthood after having, over the years, received the cumulative blessing of their parents, then they are prepared to "build their house" in the world. But without the parental blessing, a sense of self-doubt and a lack of self-worth can be so prevalent that the basic building blocks for constructing a life of happiness and self-fulfillment are simply not available. This means that the presence of the parental blessing upon one's life is a major factor in the mental and emotional health of adults.

THE WITHHELD BLESSING

Why would the parental blessing ever be withheld from a child? Certainly to ask such a question conjures up thoughts of parents who do not love their children, who are coldhearted, selfish, and irresponsible. And yet many people who struggle with a lack of blessing come from homes where their parents truly loved them and where much hard work and concern was directed toward providing for their basic needs. Why, then, is a sense of blessing often not adequately developed or communicated?

We must begin answering this question by making a crucial quali-
fying statement. It is a fact that few children ever grow into adulthood
feeling that they have fully received the parental blessing. At best a child
knows that the major aspects of his or her life are pleasing, accepted, and
affirmed. And yet there are some remaining areas where the blessing is
missing. Receiving the blessing is usually not an either-or proposition;
we have it or we don't. More often it is a matter of degree. Most of us
will leave home positioned between the diverse polarities of feeling
"mostly blessed and accepted and enjoyed by [our] parents" to the more
painful feeling of being "mostly rejected, misunderstood, and a disap-
pointing to [our] parents." Somewhere between these two extremes our
niche is carved by the wear and tear of years of family interaction. Most
of us cannot be fully blessed. That is an unrealistic expectation. We can
have the hope, though, that we will be mostly blessed.

What prevents us from being able to feel our parents' acceptance
and affirmation completely? What inhibits the blessing? Once again,
there are multiple and interconnected reasons. We will look at some
of the most basic to demonstrate how easily the blessing can be
thwarted daily by loving parents.

Discipline

One of the most difficult aspects of parenting is being a disciplinar-
ian. Even the most caring, intelligent, and sensitive of parents can be
driven to near hysteria and the fear of child abuse by a two-year-old
on a rampage or by a rebellious teenager. It is in the area of disci-
plining our children that the foundation for giving our blessing often
begins to crumble.

At its best, discipline says to the child, "I love you enough to care
for your well-being. I love you enough to place boundaries and
restrictions in your life to keep you from harm." But too often these
messages are garbled by the most well-meaning of parents into a
statement that says, "You are no good."

I am the father of three children—Drew, age eighteen, Luke, age
fifteen, and Jodi, age twelve. I love my children with a passion. Since

the first days of their lives I have prayed, "Lord, let my children grow up knowing that they have my blessing. Allow me to communicate to them that they are loved and accepted and are the joy of my life. May my blessing help them to believe in themselves and free them to be all that they can be."

Yet, so many times I have endangered their sense of blessing. I recall a moment years ago when Drew and Luke were squabbling youngsters. Drew was teasing his younger brother, as older children will do, and making Luke's life pretty tough. After repeatedly calling for an immediate cease-fire, my patience grew thin and my threat level spiked ever higher. Finally, I took Drew firmly by the arm and ushered him into the next room for a high-level conference. In a very condescending voice that had all the overtones and voice inflections of my own parents scolding me, I blurted out, "You have really been a bad boy today!" Drew's eyes dropped as if I had struck him in the face.

Now, the point is obvious. In telling Drew he was a "bad boy," I was not separating his troublesome actions from his intrinsic goodness. I did not say, "Drew, teasing Luke is forbidden." Rather, I emphatically stressed, "Drew, you are bad." I withdrew my blessing of him as a person. And trying to take back words that are destructively spoken is like trying to un-ring a bell. Said repeatedly over the course of childhood, the message is written in stone: "You are bad!"

Many people grow up in homes where no distinction is made between discipline of action and acceptance of personhood. A child who is disciplined by being told "You are a bad girl" will grow up believing it. She will not feel the hands of blessing resting on her head when it is time to leave home.

Negative Communication

We need to study more than one generation to understand a family and its communication patterns. As a pastor I have often had the opportunity to observe the communication patterns of as many as three adult generations within the same family. Intergenerational characteristics or trends usually become clear fairly quickly.

I have seen many families where the ability to affirm one another and call out each other's positive traits and gifts has been absent for at least seventy years, and possibly for much longer. Attempts at saying nice things to one another are always couched in cutting humor. "You know, despite all of his problems, Bobby's pretty smart," Dad said when his teenage son brought home a good report card. Or, in a crotchety moment, a mother might say to her daughter, "For a pretty girl with good sense, you sure do dumb things sometimes!" In short, such messages are always mixed. Affirmation is usually followed by a corresponding and neutralizing barb.

So many homes pass an unwritten legacy from one generation to another that says, "Love one another, but don't say it. Affirm one another, but cut each other down to size. Compliments should always be followed with a stout dose of humility." In that kind of environment one hand bestows the blessing while the other hand takes it away.

Though love is apparent in such families, and a fierce clan loyalty can exist between members, children emerge from such environments wondering who they really are. Are they smart or a problem— or both? Are they pretty and dumb? Straightforward communication has not been consistent. As a result the child is never sure whether he or she has received the family's blessing.

Sibling Comparisons

Another form of family communication and interaction that often confuses the giving and receiving of the blessing is what I will term *sibling comparisons*. This is apparent when two brothers hear their father proudly tell a dinner guest, "Well, Tommy is our student, and Steve is our athlete." When Tommy hears this, there is good news and bad news. Tommy is being affirmed for being a good student; he receives the blessing. But he also received this message, "Tommy's brain is better than his physical ability. He'll probably never be an athlete." And Steve hears the exact opposite: "Old Steve is pretty good with a football, but we really don't expect him to do well academically."

Tragically, the proud father loves both boys and feels that he is paying each a compliment—and he is. But the comparison of his sons has within it an inherent two-edged sword. While the blessing is bestowed on each son in one part of his life, the blessing is removed in another, and no matter how well-meaning and loving the parents are, the results are confusing.

Stress on Success

All loving parents want their children to do well in life. Most of the time their motives are good and pure: They love their children and simply wish the best for them.

Even so, motivation for encouraging one's children toward success is frequently a mixed bag. Many parents—particularly parents who received only meager portions of the parental blessing—want to live vicariously through their children. By encouraging their children to be what they wanted to be, to do what they wanted to do, to achieve where they did not have the opportunity, they are subconsciously hoping to glean their belated blessing through their children. Consequently the children are subjected to great pressures to excel.

I coach a children's soccer team, and I learned very quickly that the real egos on the line are not the children's but the parents'. So many fathers remember what it was like to be a tall, gawky, uncoordinated sixteen-year-old and to sit on the end of the bench unnoticed throughout an entire football season. When they see their six-year-old son standing on the sideline waiting his turn to play, hot adrenaline flows through their veins as they reexperience their own hurt. They want their child to be blessed in areas where they felt rejection.

I recently heard Susan talking about how she could never please her mother. Her mother was married three days after high school graduation and was nineteen years old when Susan was born. Though her mother always yearned to go to college and excel academically, the responsibilities of a young family and a meager income darkened her dreams.

When Susan was born, her mother vowed that her daughter would have everything that she had missed. From kindergarten on, great stress was placed on academic excellence. Both parents lovingly sacrificed to provide piano lessons, dance classes, and gymnastics to enhance their daughter's "well-roundedness."

But, as a sixth-grader, Susan woke up to a harsh reality. One day she scored the highest grade in her class on a math exam. Elated, she came home and proudly presented her mother with the test paper that bore the mark "98—excellent." Her mother broke into a big grin. Then with a sly twinkle in her eye, she said, "That's great, Susan! Next time make 100!"

Once again a mixed message was given. Though affirmed, Susan walked away with the dawning realization, "I'll never be good enough!" Twenty years later Susan became the talented and beautiful lawyer I told you about in the beginning of this chapter. Even though she gave every appearance of being the epitome of success and excellence, she still never felt she was good enough.

Encouraging our children to be all that they can be is a sign of mature and healthy love. It is bestowing the blessing that says, "I believe in you! I am proud of you and all that you are becoming." Yet pushed by other motivational influences, such as vicarious dream realization, parents can easily remove their hands of blessing by projecting the message "No matter what you do, it's never quite good enough." Put another way, "You are never quite good enough."

Premature Parental Loss

Sometimes the blessing can be withheld from children by loving parents as a result of loss of a parent to death or divorce. This loss affects a significant number of children in our society: In 1999, 28 percent of all American children under the age of eighteen lived in single-parent homes.[3]

When a parent leaves the home because of separation or divorce, a child will silently ask, "What's the matter with me? Am I not lovable enough to make Daddy/Mommy want to stay home? Aren't we kids important enough to make Mommy and Daddy work things out?" These are tough questions. And no matter how amiable the separation, how justified the divorce from an adult's perspective, a child will usually feel personal rejection. Again, loving parents did not want this to happen. But situations converged that resulted in a child feeling, "I'm not good enough." And the parental blessing begins to slip from the child's life.

The loss of a parent by death can be equally debilitating. I can speak to this from personal experience. When I was fourteen my father had a heart attack and died. His death impinged upon me at a difficult and transitional stage of adolescent development.

In the days immediately preceding his death, we had been locked into some very difficult and intense battles over authority—natural conflict issues for teenagers. I had wanted to grow my hair long, like the Beatles. He insisted I get a haircut. I had not wanted to join the family on vacation and miss high school football practice. Despite a furious argument, he demanded that I go.

On the day before he died we had the most intense encounter we had ever experienced over what he called my "attitude problem." I know now that we were engaged in very normal transition adjustments of the adolescent years. Inevitably, for a short while, we were adversaries. Neither of us could give the other our blessing.

And then, before we could work things out, he died. And although he didn't intend to, he took his blessing with him. Down deep I knew he loved me intensely and was proud of me, and, for the most part, we had a good and mutually close relationship. But still, he died before our emotional bridge could be mended. The blessing was withheld, and I felt abandoned by my father.

THE DRIVE TO FILL THE VOID

Now to get to the heart of our discussion: The biggest problem of not receiving (or partially receiving) the blessing is that we cannot endure the hollow ache of unworthiness within us. We are driven by an insatiable need to fill the void with something. So we set out to get somebody else to give us a blessing.

Susan, the lawyer, never felt that she fully received her mother's blessing. And so she married a young man who had a natural ability to be openly affirming and supportive. Yet there was one problem. Just as Susan's mother was seldom satisfied when Susan excelled—holding out for an A+ when Susan made an A—so now Susan found that her need for affirmation and blessing could rarely be met. Though more affirming than most marriage partners, her husband could never support her enough. She constantly questioned his sincerity, sloughed off his compliments, and, paradoxically, felt unappreciated. This tension put a tremendous strain on their marriage. Both husband and wife felt frustrated, misunderstood, and unappreciated. Susan simply could not vicariously receive her mother's blessing from her husband or anyone else.

I also remember well when I first came face to face with my own futile attempts to obtain my deceased father's blessing. As a teenager without a father, I always knew that I held older men's opinions of me as being very important. How my athletic coaches related to me was of paramount importance. Later, a kind or encouraging word from a college professor would really make my day. But there was nothing obviously unusual about this. Every teenager tries to impress the coach, and most college students yearn for praise from their professor.

However, when I graduated from seminary and was employed as an associate pastor at the First Baptist Church of Athens, Georgia, my confrontation with my need for the paternal blessing slowly crept into view. One of the inciting incidents that brought it into focus was innocent enough.

We had just completed our annual Youth Week. I had worked hard and had planned and directed a creative worship service, conducted a weekend retreat, sweated through endless games of volleyball and basketball, and orchestrated social events every night. The week was a tremendous success, and I felt good.

Sunday night, at the conclusion of the final activities, I found myself closing up the church. Out in the parking lot the senior minister, Jon Appleton, was talking to the last parent to leave. I turned off the lights and remained in the shadows of the church, waiting to speak to Jon alone.

Deep inside, I knew I didn't want to talk to Jon: I wanted Jon to talk to me. I desperately wanted him to say how good the week was, to compliment me on how hard I had worked and what a gift I had with youth. And so I waited in the shadows for his blessing.

Finally, the conversation was concluded and Jon walked to his car. I hailed him and walked toward him. We both were exhausted. After some small talk, Jon yawned, slapped the top of his car good-naturedly, and said, "It's been a long week! Let's go home!" And so we did. Each driving in opposite directions.

As I pulled out of the parking lot, I could feel the tension bubbling up within me. I tasted a strange concoction of anger, hurt, depression, and grief all churning together. I began to rage against Jon's seeming insensitivity. He didn't even tell me I had done a decent job. Stopping at a traffic light, I slammed my fist into the dashboard and felt tears sting my eyes.

Though I was directing my anger toward Jon, I was perceptive enough to sense that the problem was much deeper. Sure, I wanted Jon to affirm my work. Any young man would. And I knew that Jon did. But the intensity of my tears and smoldering anger betrayed the fact that the source of my feelings were much deeper. I somehow sensed that I was unfairly transferring my need for a father's blessing upon Jon. And I wanted from Jon what he—or anyone else— could not give me. Only Al Walker could give me that blessing. And he was dead.

Again, we must look to one of the central tenets of the Old Testament blessing. Only the father could bestow the blessing upon the child. And from our understanding of psychology, we know that only the mother and father can bestow the parental blessing upon their children. When this blessing is partial or nonexistent, a child can go through life insatiably demanding from others a blessing they cannot give. Such demands and expectations, when not openly recognized, can destroy friendships, marriages, and professional relationships. For to demand the blessing from those who cannot give it is to ensure a constant feeling of frustration, disappointment, and resentment within significant relationships.

COMING TO PEACE
WITH OUR BLESSING

What can we do to relieve the tension of and gain our freedom from this double bind? How can we who yearn and strive for the blessing obtain it when others cannot give it to us?

There is no one nice and easy answer, but a combination of approaches and solutions can bolster—though not eradicate or "cure"—our flagging sense of self-worth and self-esteem.

To Recognize a Common Malady

First, to confront our struggle with the lack of blessing, we must come to see that most people live with this problem in varying degrees. National studies have found that as many as one-third of Americans are plagued by a low sense of self-worth. In fact, many behavioral scientists consider low self-esteem to be the number one psychological problem in our society today.[4] At the root of this phenomenon of low self-esteem, I believe, is the incomplete parental blessing, for we receive our primary sense of self-worth from our parents.

Now, the problem with many people who wrestle with feeling "I'm not good enough" is their assumption, in spite of national statistics, that they are all alone in their struggle. As we look at the smooth exterior of other people, we are certain they could not possibly share our feelings of inadequacy, shame, insecurity, embarrassment, and perhaps self-loathing. And the more we are convinced that our struggle is unique, the more tightly we press down and try not to show our pain.

And yet counselors, therapists, and ministers, who have the unique privilege of looking deeply into the lives of others, know that many people struggle with feeling "unblessed." And if everyone could see things from the counselor's vantage point, they would feel better about their own struggle. They would know then that they are not weird, neurotic, deficient, or warped. As we face up to the truth that we're all in this together—we are all struggling to obtain the missing blessing—we can move on to face our need instead of attempting to suppress and hide our problem. We are then free to be victors and not victims.

The novelist James Baldwin once said that "not everything that is faced can be changed; but nothing can be changed until it is faced."[5] As we face our inner terror because we feel unblessed, we can take positive steps to better cope with our situation in healthy ways.

Parents Are Not Perfect

Once we have accepted the fact that we are among millions of people who did not receive their parents' full blessing, then another truth becomes apparent: Parents are not perfect people. They were incapable of giving us their total blessing no matter how much they wanted to.

During my twenties, as I grew into independence, I did my share of criticizing my parents for what I considered to be their errors in parenting me. As I confronted areas of my life where I felt insecure, it was easy to blame my instability on Mom and Dad. For the most part this process of "kicking the barn door" was healthy, even though many times I was far from correct and objective.

But now I am fifty years old, and something new has happened. I am the father of three children and the tables have turned. Suddenly it is I who is to give the blessing, and I am finding myself struggling with this task. In fact I often pray that I will have the good grace to be able to do as well as my parents.

In her brilliant book *Necessary Losses,* Judith Viorst speaks of coming to terms with the inherent limitations of parenthood. She writes:

> Indeed, it has often been said, that in becoming parents ourselves, we now understand what our mother and father went through and thus can no longer blame and denounce them, as once we could easily do, for all that we have suffered at their hands. Parenthood can be a constructive developmental phase in

which we heal some of the wounds of our own childhood. It also may allow us to recast our old perceptions of that childhood in less alienated, more reconciling ways.[6]

So, to objectively appraise the task of parenting—particularly where we experience parenting firsthand—is to face up to the fact that there are no perfect parents. And because there are no perfect parents, there can be no perfect blessings. Consequently, to mature as an adult is to recognize that we all have scars from childhood and we must accept them. And Viorst concludes, "in midlife, in those years from thirty-five to forty-five or fifty, we learn that many hopes remain unredeemed. There is plenty that we wanted, and did not receive, from our parents. It is time to know and accept that we never will."[7]

However, such recognition should not in itself be discouraging or fatalistic. Rather, when we realize that our parents were limited and that they struggled to bless us imperfectly as we also now struggle to bless our children, we enter into a potentially liberating experience. For we can now realize that we are not flawed people because we did not receive the full blessing. The process of giving the blessing was itself inherently limited and deficient.

Building on this idea, Howard M. Halpern writes, "It is crucial to begin to accept that your parents' not loving you [or blessing you] is a statement about them and not about you. In other words, it bespeaks a defect in their ability to love rather than a defect in your lovability."[8] Without doubt this can be a liberating insight.

I have reflected upon my relationship with my father in recent years, and I have begun to realize that I actually had his blessing all along. But it took blowing it a few times with my children, experiencing the frustration of trying my best to be a loving parent and only partially succeeding, before I could understand my father's blessing upon me in a different light. Sure, some scar tissue remains. But, with this new realization, the hurt is beginning to fade. I am discovering for myself what my mother always told me and I could not hear until now: "He only loved you, son. He only loved you."

Most of our parents tried very hard to bless us. But they were not perfect. And neither are we.

The Blessing from Within

Even as we mature to the point where we understand that our parents were incapable of fully blessing us, there remains an aching void within. We are driven then to try to go outside of ourselves and "earn" the blessing from others; to fill our emptiness with their praise. We feel that if we can be successful or famous, be a public servant, an outstanding athlete, an exceptional minister, or a gifted artist, then those we want desperately to please will give us their blessing. But we cannot "earn" the blessing; when we strive to earn it, we become aware that we are being affirmed for what we *do* and not for who we *are*.

Many of the most hollow and empty people are the most famous people. Their desire to be blessed, to finally "be somebody," has driven them to climb the ladder of success to great heights and at great expense. And yet when their picture is in newspapers and on billboards, when their autograph is requested and they see the reflection of their own face mirrored in the ogling eyes of admirers, they realize, "These people don't even know who I am. They love me for who they think I am, for what I represent." Such realization is incredibly painful and reinforces the awareness that "I am not blessed."

Great achievers—famous or unknown—find themselves in the same boat. When their work is done, the project completed, a promotion or bonus earned, they go home empty-handed, realizing, "What I do has been affirmed. But not who I am."

And so when we find ourselves exhausted and teetering on the top rung of our success ladder, the truth crashes in, "The blessing cannot come from outside of me. It can only come from within."

This means that the choice is ours. We can join old Captain Ahab and be driven to sail the seven seas in a vain attempt to capture the elusive blessing and destroy ourselves in the process. Or we can call off the destructive pursuit and come to grips with our situation, knowing that the portion of the blessing we are missing can only come from within us.

The Power of Friendship

To say that the missing portion of the blessing can only come from within sounds profound. Yet such a statement throws most of us into deep confusion. Indeed, as I write these words, I feel as though I have just told a lonely man to go hug himself. It cannot be done. A hug can have warmth and meaning only when it comes from someone else. And for the blessing to be "grasped within" always requires the helping hands of others.

Yet we have just concluded that the blessing cannot be earned or gained from others. And this is paradoxically true. However, true friends can help us to look deeply within ourselves and realize that we are blessed. Friends cannot give us the blessing, but they can help us to realize that we have been worthy of the blessing all along.

A true friend is one who likes you for who you are. There is a natural chemistry between you. A true friendship is not based on "what you can do for me" or "what I have done for you." True friendship always revolves around a simple statement, which my son Drew used to say when he was two: "I like you!" And that is why true friendship is so rare and precious. It cannot be contrived or forced or earned.

Though such friendships are rare, most of us over the years have managed to forge from the heat of life a few true friends. And they can be an invaluable catalyst to help us receive our own blessing. Friends can hold a mirror before our face that will help us see our-selves as we really are.

Recently a friend invited me to lunch. We have not known each other for very long, but there has been a strong sense of that chem-istry that bonds true friends together. In the middle of lunch he looked at me and said, "I don't know how to say this. It makes me feel a little awkward. But our friendship is important to me. And I don't want our professional relationship to interfere with that. I like you because I just like you. And I want you to know that."

I could feel the blood rushing to my face. His words felt very good. I was moved by his honesty and affirmation of me. And I also devoured his words like a starving man being offered a meal. But, paradoxically, something within me wanted to protest. As I groped for words and tried to reply, I almost found myself saying, "Well, I really appreciate you liking me. However, you just don't know who I am. Allow some time for the paint to fade." But, happily, I resisted that response and choked out an awkward, "Thank you."

People who have not adequately received the blessing have great difficulty accepting the compliments, praise, or affirmation that could help them see they are worthy of the blessing. Though we hear the words, we are like people who have surgically received a stomach bypass. We swallow the food of affirmation given by others, but it circumvents our emotional stomachs, and we receive no nurture and no strengthening from the loving acceptance given by friends.

All of us who struggle with insecurity and lack of blessing must come to recognize this and consciously refuse to deny and reject the affirmation of friends. We must reprogram ourselves to listen to and accept their praise.

I remember when this truth hit me some years ago. I was listening spellbound to the talented author and priest John Powell address an assembly of ministers. He was talking about how difficult it is for ministers to allow themselves to receive love and affirmation from others. With intensity he shouted at us, "Look at how often people love you. If they do, are they crazy?"[9]

This was the slap in the face that brought me to my senses. If my friends really love me—and undeniably they do—then are they crazy? No, they're not. Indeed, if anybody is crazy, it's me for not accepting their love and affirmation.

The Support of the Mentor

Alongside the true friend stands another who can help us reach inside ourselves and accept the fact that we are blessed. This important figure is called "the mentor."

In his remarkable book *The Seasons of a Man's Life,* Daniel J. Levinson introduced me to the concept of the mentor. A mentor is usually an older person, a person of experience and streetwise wisdom who has seniority in the world a younger man or woman is entering. The mentor voluntarily takes the younger person in and serves as teacher, model, and perhaps advisor. The mentor may serve as a sponsor to help the protégé advance and receive opportunities for personal and professional growth.

Perhaps more important, however, the mentor serves as "an analogue in adulthood of the 'good enough' parent for the child. He fosters the young adult's development by believing in him, sharing the youthful dream and giving it his blessing."[10]

More than anything else, a mentor is an older figure in your life who believes in you and encourages you. He or she is not a surrogate parent or a peer. And his or her praise and support is not carte blanche. The mentor can be constructively critical and demanding as well. But above all, the mentor communicates affirmation and support and believes in you.

Mentors are not easily found. They are a gift. And like true friendships they depend on natural chemistry, which cannot be forced or contrived. But fortunate is the person who has encountered a mentor or a series of mentors in life.

I have been privileged to have several mentors during my adult years. Each of them has been different and unique and has affected me profoundly in different parts of my life. But they all have sounded one common theme that helped me look within myself and claim my own blessing—"I believe in you and encourage your life's dream." Though they could not give me the parental blessing, they held a mirror before my face and helped me claim it for myself.

In *A Place For You,* noted Swiss psychiatrist Paul Tournier writes, "How many great artists would have never become so without an obscure master [mentor], whose name history has forgotten? The confidence shown in them by their master, quite as much as his teaching, has helped them give of their best."[11] Certainly the confidence of others can help us look within and grasp the blessing that is ours. We must hear again the words of John Powell: "Look at how often people love you. If they do, are they crazy?" Mentors aren't crazy. They challenge us to see ourselves as they do.

The Love of God

Though true friends and mentors are important for helping us look inside and see that we are blessed, there is one more relationship that is crucial in this process—more crucial than any other. And that is our relationship with our creator, God.

Certainly the Bible teaches that God has given men and women His blessing. In the Genesis story of creation, when God had finished making the physical world and all that lives in it, he said unreservedly, "It is good" (Gen. 1:31). This means that men and women have had God's blessing upon their lives from the very beginning. Even though we sin and separate ourselves from God, we still retain God's blessing.

Moving from the global and metaphysical nature of the book of Genesis to the more concrete and historically tangible life of Jesus Christ, we again find the blessing of God being reconfirmed.

We do not know much about Jesus' family life. We can only surmise that his father, Joseph, died after Jesus was twelve and before the beginning of his public ministry at age thirty. We know nothing of Jesus' relationship to Joseph or if, as a young man, he ever formally received his father's blessing. However, what we do know is that when the adult Jesus referred to his relationship with God, he called him "Abba," a Hebrew child's word of endearment, which literally means "Daddy."

The reference to God as "Abba" was unprecedented in Jewish literature before the time of Jesus. Indeed, Jesus' reference to God as "Daddy" was not only novel and unique to him, it was also heard as blasphemous by many of his contemporaries. To "lower" God to this earthly form of intimacy was unheard of.[12]

And yet this unique reference to God gives us more insight into Jesus' theology than any other. As the oldest son in a Jewish family, the one who was to receive the blessing from his father, Jesus looked to

God and transferred this same relational idea of father to God. Jesus knew that God was a God of tender, intimate, "fatherly" love and acceptance.

Correspondingly the Gospels of Matthew, Mark, and Luke all agree that at Jesus' baptism—his moment of "leaving home"—God's Spirit communicated to him the marvelous affirmation, "Thou art my beloved Son, in thee. I am well-pleased" (Mark 1:11; Luke 3:22; Matt. 3:17). The theme of blessing continues from Adam unto Jesus.

So we can see that there is a God-given blessing that supersedes even our parental blessing. For God comes to each person within whom he has breathed the breath of life and he says, "You are good! . . . You are my beloved son or daughter in whom I am well-pleased."

Even though Jesus was the first and only person who was able to live totally "in the image of God" and thus authenticate the blessing of his Father, we all receive God's blessing. Whether we squander that blessing or try to authenticate it is told by the course and the history of our lives. But as with the Prodigal Son, that blessing is never removed. We may go to a far-off land. We may even travel so far away we arrive in hell. But we cannot eradicate the fact that God created us "good," and that he has given us his blessing. Whether we choose to accept God's blessing and try to authenticate it, or reject it and move "East of Eden," the blessing is ours to be claimed.

As I finished writing the last paragraph, I put my pencil down and walked out into the night. This week I am staying at a friend's cottage on the coast of South Carolina. As I ambled down the beach I gazed at the brilliance of the stars. The same stars that Adam saw, that Jesus saw, that my grandfather and father saw. I was overcome by awe and mystery.

Somewhere up there is a Spirit of Love we call God who knows my every thought and action and still loves me. If somehow I can realize this a little more, if over the years of my life I can slowly absorb a truth greater than the universe, then maybe I won't have to work so hard, please others so much, feel so empty, and constantly be driven to seek the blessing. The blessing is within me. It's within you. It is ours to accept. And our blessing can set us free to experience contentment.

Chapter Two

LET GO OF
SECRETS AND SHAME

B OBBY AND I WERE THE SAME AGE, and we had graduated from high school the same year. Yet life had dealt us different cards. While I was forced to wear a ridiculous beanie during freshman initiation at a sheltered college, he buckled the chin strap of a steel army helmet and learned to march and slither through the mud of boot camp. Later, while I went to autumn football games and dated pretty girls, he completed two rugged tours of duty as an Army Ranger in Vietnam.

A decade later, I met Bobby's parents when I became their pastor. But I had never seen Bobby until he showed up one night on my doorstep, drunk and crying. He said he needed help.

As we talked, he poured out years of pain and struggle. He had been through two marriages and two divorces and had two children to show for it all. He had held all sorts of jobs, but none longer than a year. The one major thread of destruction woven throughout the garment of his adult life was a drug and alcohol abuse problem. He couldn't kick it. A marijuana habit begun in the hellish jungles of Vietnam had grown into a tiger of cocaine, alcohol, and heroin addiction.

I knew that I was not clinically qualified to deal with the specialized problem of substance abuse, so I began to look for treatment options for Bobby. Finally I was able to get him into a six-week residential rehabilitation program. With one suitcase in hand, Bobby walked all alone through the doors of the treatment center and began the biggest battle of his life.

Five weeks later he called me. He asked me to accompany his parents to his final session with his therapist. He said he needed my support.

On the day of Bobby's discharge I met his parents at the treatment center for the exit session. They were not the only ones who were nervous. I was tense as well. I looked into their aging eyes and saw they were afraid to get their hopes up. Too many times they had picked Bobby up, tended his wounds, brushed him off, and started all over again. And each time they had been disappointed. Would things be any different this time?

Bobby's therapist, Ellen, met us with a smile. "Glad you could make it," she said. "I think he needs you today." Ushering us down a no-nonsense hallway, she directed us into her office. Chairs were arranged in a circle and we sat down. As she asked us if we cared for coffee, Bobby shuffled quietly in. Still a little gaunt and pale, he hugged his parents, and his dad patted him affectionately on the back. I embraced him, too. And then we sat down.

To break the ice Ellen began to tell us about Bobby's therapy. And then she said, "Bobby, why don't you share with us what you've experienced here? What's important to you?"

He began slowly at first, haltingly. But as he warmed to the task his words flowed more smoothly. He spoke of the encounter groups, what he felt his fellow patients had in common. And then, like an old victrola winding down, he talked more guardedly and slowly grew quiet.

Seconds of silence began to feel like minutes of pain. I grew uncomfortable, shifted my legs, and fought the urge to speak. Finally Ellen broke the uneasy quiet. She said softly, "Bobby, we've learned that we are as safe as our secrets."

Bobby slumped over, placed his face in his hands, and began to sob and tremble. His mother leaned forward as if to reach out to him, and then thought better of it. For what seemed like an hour but was only a minute, we heard the sounds of wrenching emotion—the heaving sobs of inner dissonance and agonizing indecision.

As spontaneously as it had begun, Bobby's sobbing stopped. Looking up through layers of tears, he spat out the words, "I killed children, Momma. And women. And I've got a baby in Da Nang, too." At last the secret was out.

In a few moments Bobby told us how his platoon had set an ambush one dark night on a jungle path. When the "enemy" came, they had opened fire. And when the shooting was over, the sound that could be heard was not the moans of wounded men. It was the screams of several dying and mangled village families. Fearing a counter-ambush, his patrol had melted into the jungle, leaving the whimpering cries of children pleading in the night.

From that point on Bobby went downhill. He began to numb his pain with alcohol and later with drugs. And then in a vain attempt to bring warmth into the death-filled coldness of his own life, he had shacked up with a Vietnamese barmaid. She had become pregnant before the end of his first tour, so he had volunteered for another year. Then everything fell apart.

American troops were withdrawn. Bobby was ordered home. The North Vietnamese Army moved south and Saigon fell. For years he had not heard a word from the mother of his little girl. He lived in agony imagining his daughter as a little street child with his own blue eyes.

Until that day he had never told a soul. How would his conservative parents react? And what if he had told either wife? It was better to keep quiet. Vietnam was another world away. Another life. A bygone day. A horrid nightmare.

I realized I had been holding my breath. I looked across at the stunned faces of Bobby's parents. Slowly they got up, walked over, and embraced their son. A relationship divided by a wedge of secrecy and shame had just been breached. A demon had been cast out. A cancer removed. And I sat there exhausted

I have often thought about that electric moment. And I will never forget the therapist's words: "We are as safe as our secrets." She nailed me with a phrase that has all the resonance of profound truth and authenticity. In my life I have discovered her words to be true.

SECRETS CAN BE HEALTHY

So many things in life are paradoxical—that is, the same truth or entity can be both good and bad. Secrets are such a paradox, for they are two-edged swords: They can defend us from great harm, but, at the same time, secrets can sever our own emotional jugular vein.

How, on the one hand, are secrets good and healthy? In a little book entitled *Secrets,* Paul Tournier writes of how important and essential secrets are to the healthy development and growth of children, adolescents, and even adults. Tournier points out that without the privilege of secrecy, a child cannot break out of an overly dependent relationship with parents—particularly the mother—and become in a true sense an individual. Tournier writes, "It is to the extent that he has secrets from his parents that he gains an awareness of self; it is to the extent that he becomes free to keep his secrets from them that he gets an awareness of being distinct from them, of having his own individuality, of being a person."[1] This simply means that for a child to emerge as a distinct individual who has worth and freedom, he or she must be allowed—even encouraged—to have secrets.

Yet most parents are threatened by their children's secrets. They perceive their silent concealment as subtle dishonesty. And at an ever-deepening level, they correctly comprehend that their child is growing up and becoming separate from them. Most parents want to slow this inevitable process of separation and so they fight against the severing symbol of secrecy.

Consequently it is difficult for parents to understand that secretive tendencies can be healthy. Without the freedom of secrecy a child's life will be damaged, and growth into healthy autonomy will be stunted.

I remember a moment years ago when I experienced a delightful Halloween at our home. My youngest son, Luke, was two and a half— just old enough to really enjoy such an event. With Drew dressed as a pirate, and Luke as a *Sesame Street* character named Bert, we walked up and down our street ringing doorbells and collecting candy from smiling neighbors. It was one of those rich, wide-eyed experiences of childhood.

Later that night, as both boys grew green around the gills from having eaten too much of their loot, down came the parental decree, "No more candy tonight, boys." And, of course, there was the immediate protest of shrill little voices decrying the reining in of their freedom to get sick. But protest or not, it was time for a good thing to come to an end.

The next day, when I came home from work, I walked down the hall to hang up my coat. As I neared the closet I heard a strange thumping inside. My first thought was that the cat had been trapped again. And then I saw a candy wrapper jutting out from under the door. I began to grin. Luke was at it again. He had taken his Halloween treat bag into the secrecy of the closet and was having a good old time.

Looking at my watch, I started to throw the door open and flip on my recorded parental tape that was handed down to me from my mother concerning the perils of eating sweets before mealtime. But with my hand on the doorknob, I began to chuckle. I could see in my mind that little blond rascal huddling inside, holding his breath, hiding his candy, and forgetting the evidence of chocolate on his face. I remembered the richness of doing similar things in my childhood, and I quietly walked away. Some things are more important than supper. And a child's right to privacy—within reason—is one of those things.

Now, of course, it's going to be a little harder next year when Luke's sixteen and driving. When the hall closet has become the big wide world and the treat bag contains all the flavors of wine, women, and song, then I'm going to be more prone to wipe away my grin and attempt to fling open the door. And there will be times when I should. But the truth will remain the same: for a child to mature and become an individual, privacy and the right to secrets—indeed, failure—is essential.

And so it is in adulthood. I recently reread George Orwell's *1984*. I cringed at the thought of living in a society where individualism is taken away, where there is no privacy, and where "Big Brother" knows everything. I value wearing clothes that symbolize my privacy. I value the four walls of my house and a lock on my door, a bank account with a personal identification number, and secluded memories that I and those I love cherish. I relish the moments in worship when the organ stops playing and the preacher quits speaking and we are called to silent prayer. Life without secrets would be hell. And I am glad that, in his wisdom, God granted us a secrecy known only unto him.

SECRETS CAN BE DESTRUCTIVE

Secrets are healthy, but they can also be destructive. A small kernel of secrecy buried deep within the soul can fester and swell until it becomes a malignant growth, sapping vitality and threatening life. And so we are left asking the question, "What makes the crucial difference between whether a secret is healthy and leads to maturity and freedom or is cancerous and leads to disease?" The primary difference to me is a word called *shame*.

Shameful Secrets

Secrets that are healthy are the beautiful wrapping paper around precious objects and moments, the secret that envelops things we treasure and are not ashamed of. Once again I turn to Tournier's wisdom:

> Yes, secrecy is like a strongbox where we can piously keep treasures: some remembrances of some beautiful past, quite finished; some photos carefully wrapped up and locked away, some manuscript begun with enthusiasm and which never dared confront publication, and which stays there, with its nostalgia, in the bottom of a drawer; some painting that the amateur artist has never been able to finish; some intimate diary with innumerable notebooks. . . . Yes, a certain secrecy, to just the right extent, ought to enclose every precious thing, every precious experience, so that it can mature and bear fruit.[2]

Yet, though the amateur artist has not finished the painting and still has it veiled, it is not veiled by deep and morbid shame. Rather, it is veiled like a cask of fine wine fermenting—waiting for the years to pass, the fermentation to take place, before the delicious vintage is shared with others.

But so many secrets are encased by no other substance than the black tar paper of shame. And so we ask, "What exactly is this shame that transforms wine into poison?"

In recent years psychologists have come to recognize that shame is one of the master emotions that influence all other emotions.[3] This discovery was late in coming because so much emphasis has been placed on its sibling emotion, guilt. Yet shame and guilt, though intimately related, are distinctly different.

Guilt is regret and remorse owing to an action or attitude. Shame is much more than this. Shame is guilt compounded a thousand times. Shame is the grief of the loss of our own self-esteem; the death of self-respect. Shame sinks its roots deeper than guilt and goes to one's basic sense of goodness. It begins to distort and denigrate a person's basic concept of selfhood and worth.

Shame is such a well-guarded emotion that Dr. Paul Ekman, a psychologist at the University of California at San Francisco and an expert on facial expressions, reports, "Shame may be one of the only emotions for which no facial expression has evolved . . . Turning away or hiding the face in some way are the only objective signs of shame."[4]

When shame is allowed to grow over a period of time, it can result in a deep and silent sense of self-loathing and a profound feeling that one is not worthy of love or respect. This was true in Bobby's case; he felt far more than guilt over his unwitting participation in the slaying of women and children. When this was compounded by the birth of his child whom he later "deserted," the raw shame began to gnaw at his soul.

Because shame demands our agonized silence and even neutralizes our facial expressions, Bobby found himself driven and alone in a torture chamber where he was both victim and sadistic inquisitor. He numbed his pain with alcohol and drugs. Others numb their pain by workaholism, zealous "do-gooding," depression, and flights into fantasy.

Such blights of shame can engulf whole families. Marilyn Mason, a family therapist at the University of Minnesota Medical School, has reported that entire families can share debilitating feelings of shame over such events as suicide, bankruptcy, child abuse, or alcoholism. According to Mason, "The family's implicit rule becomes not to talk about painful life experiences of all kinds."[5]

In his powerful novel *The Prince of Tides*, Pat Conroy weaves the story of a family raised in the marshes of the coastal plains of South Carolina. Isolated in a shrimping village, the family falls prey to the unstable husband and father, who cannot control his sporadic impulses to fly into rages and physically assault his wife and children. Yet his wife, masking her personal feelings of inferiority behind a fierce sense of pride, demands that the children keep their struggle strictly to themselves. No one is to be told. No help is to be sought. It is a family affair.

Conroy shows how this kernel of family shame grows to be a monster that attempts to enslave and devour all the children in their later adult years, long after the beatings have ended. In a statement of poignant insight, one of the children says, "We are a family of well-kept secrets and they all nearly end up killing us."[6]

That is the tragedy of secrets shrouded in shame. They all nearly end up killing us.

THE ANATOMY OF DEATH

Exactly how do these shameful secrets lead to our emotional dying? There are at least three interrelated steps.

Fears Grow Bigger Than Life

First, by keeping a shameful and fear-producing event a tightly guarded secret, the fear and its trappings begin to grow to exaggerated proportions. It exhibits the dynamics of the fabled mouse scaring the lion.

When I was a little boy I used to visit my dad's office. He had a paperweight on his desk that fascinated me. It was a glass sphere filled with water. Inside the glass ball was a winter scene—a red and white plastic house and a snowman. When I picked up the paperweight and shook it, small flakes of snow would begin flurrying inside this miniature winter world.

One day, as my little hand grasped this marvel and shook it, the paperweight flew from my fingers and shattered on the tile floor. Frightened and embarrassed, I bent down to pick up the pieces. As I did, I was amazed at an unexpected discovery.

Sitting on the desk, the house and snowman had seemed so big and prominent inside the watery world of the enclosed glass ball. Indeed the glass and water had magnified them to twice their actual size. But now, with the glass broken and the water puddled all about, the little plastic pieces were no bigger than my thumbnail. My three-year-old mind was amazed at this first-time discovery of optical illusion.

And yet my adult mind is still frequently duped by this same concept in the arena of psychic illusion. When shameful secrets are kept tightly sealed within the watery sphere of our minds, the things we fear are magnified to mammoth proportions. Bobby had been certain that if he told his parents about Vietnam, they would disown him. Friends would call him a cold-blooded murderer and shun him. And heaven help him if either of his wives had known about his lost little girl in Da Nang. And so the fear grew and multiplied until the demon was Legion.

But there was even a bigger fear: his fear of himself. Could he live with himself? Or would his own anxiety and shame drive him crazy or to suicide or to harming someone else? When his mind started thinking these frantic thoughts, he'd reach for the bottle or the needle. And slowly the world would fade into "safe" oblivion.

What Bobby was soon to discover is that when the glass was shattered and his terrible secrets were let out, his biggest fears shrank, shriveled up. His parents loved him. I understood and fully accepted him. And, most important, his fears of "cracking up" began to dissipate.

As his therapist so wisely saw, Bobby had to learn experientially that "we are as safe as our secrets." And when shameful secrets are suppressed and repressed, little mice become monsters that set the bravest of lions to flight.

Destructive Behavior Is Repeated

A second dangerous consequence of withholding our secrets of shame is that such secrecy compels us to repeat destructive behavior. In Bobby's case his own personality traits led him to cope repeatedly with his fears and the agony of shame through alcohol and drug addiction.

Now, Bobby was no dummy. His intelligence level was higher than average. He was a sensitive person and, when he was himself, Bobby was a likable fellow. Make no mistake about it, he genuinely wanted to get well. He hated his addiction. In addition Bobby was strong willed; he had been strong enough to be a Ranger and endure the rigors of Vietnam.

But there was one thing stronger than Bobby's resolve to get well. And that was his fear of the monsters of shame magnified to enormous proportions in the secrecy of his mind. And until these secrets were out, talked about, and exposed to the light of day, Bobby was doomed to repeat destructive behavior.

How many workaholics want to stop for a few weeks and relax but can't find the courage to do so? How many food-addicted people truly long to quit eating but are enslaved by the table? How many people compulsively repeat destructive sexual affairs, embezzle money, or practice child abuse? The behavior patterns—the coping mechanisms—are different, but the driving mechanism is the same. Repressed feelings of shame lead to the slavery of repeated destructive behavior.

Until we can find the courage to reveal the secret that has caused our shame, we cannot stop the destructive behavior. And yet most people want to handle their problem in the reverse order. They want to focus on the destructive behavior first and disregard the secret. It cannot be done; freedom won't come that way. Until the secrets are spoken, the behavior leading to death will continue. Once again, "We are as safe as our secrets."

We Are Doomed to Isolation

Our secrets of shame incarcerate us in a prison of isolation. No matter how much others like us, reach out to us, and befriend us, our inner response is always the same: "If they really knew me, they would not like me."

Bobby had been married twice. In both marriages there was genuine love and affection between partners. However, over time, Bobby's repeated pattern of destructive behavior wreaked havoc in the relationship. Perhaps most important, in neither marriage did Bobby feel that he was loved.

As long as Bobby saw himself as a murderer and a heartless, deserting father, he could not believe his wife or anyone else when they said, "I love you." In fact every time someone said, "I love you," he felt lonelier. And intimacy quickly eroded away.

In an earlier book, *Where the Rivers Flow,* I tell a story of how the death of my father, my family's traumatic uprooting, and my normal teenage adjustments brought me to a time in my early twenties when I was going through much emotional pain.[7] I had many secrets locked inside of me. There were feelings not only of grief, but of deep shame. I began to experience depression and anxiety attacks.

At this point the monsters in my own mind were really magnified. I feared a nervous breakdown and was shamed by what I considered to be my own emotional weakness. Had my personality been oriented toward addiction, or if I had been surrounded by the drug world of Vietnam, I could have gone down the same road that Bobby traveled.

By the grace of God and the advice of wise friends, the pain of my shameful secrets brought me to the door of a wise pastoral counselor named Wayne Oates. He encouraged me to break the "glass ball" and let my secrets out.

I have a vivid memory of walking out of Dr. Oates's office one afternoon after I had really confessed all. As I walked to my car feeling twenty pounds lighter, I remember saying, "I'm not sure I can face Dr. Oates next week without blushing. But it sure is good to know that if a Mack truck hits me on the way home, at least I know that one person in this world really knows Scott Walker." That was such a liberating feeling, and it was the first step toward a rapid recovery of emotional and spiritual health.

Until we tell our secrets, we will be locked into the terrible prison of isolation. For even when people attempt to love us, we will say, "If they really knew me, secrets and all, they would not like me."

AN IMPORTANT WORD OF CAUTION

If I were to end this chapter here, I am afraid I would leave you in a very perilous position. Up to this point I could be understood as saying, "Hang all your dirty linen out for all the world to see. Become an emotional exhibitionist. Put down this book right now and go tell your spouse about that affair you had five years ago. Keep no secrets from anybody." No, that is emphatically not what I am saying.

Once again, let's refer to Bobby. When he came to that place in his life where he realized he could go no further without help, the first thing he did was consult his family's pastor. And his pastor, after hearing his story over the course of several weeks, placed him in the care of a specialist.

It was only after six weeks of intense therapy that a psychologist and Bobby came to the mutual decision that in order for Bobby to come to health, he needed to tell three important people in his life his shameful secret: his father, his mother, and his pastor. And over time he learned that we loved the real Bobby—perhaps more than ever before. Consequently there was no need for him to share his secret with anybody else.

Bobby later felt he could share his story more openly. Over the years, he has frequently helped other people mired in addictions. And, through the confessional support of Alcoholics Anonymous, he has completed years of sobriety.

The important lesson to be learned is that when we finally decide to confront the monsters of our shameful secrets, we should first consult a professional—a pastor, a psychologist, or a psychiatrist. There are several reasons for this.

Confidentiality

One of the greatest concerns of people who are first beginning to realize the importance of verbalizing their destructive secrets is the need for total confidentiality. It is imperative for you to know that when you first confess your story it will go no further.

Although family and friends may have our most immediate trust, there is always the fear that in a weak moment, or totally by accident, they might spill the beans. For this reason the best source of confidentiality is a pastor or a psychologist who is professionally accountable to sustain confidentiality of all conversations.

Objectivity and Expertise

When a person becomes willing to divulge painful secrets and literally put his life in another's hands, that person needs to know that the counselor can listen with total objectivity and can also interact with professional expertise.

My family members love me intensely, but their love and our interdependent relationship keeps them from listening to me with objectivity. I must frequently second-guess their response to me when their welfare is so intimately tied up with my own.

Similarly, if ever I should need brain surgery, you can bet that I am going to select a skilled and qualified neurosurgeon, and not my tennis partner. When I begin to deal with some of the most carefully guarded and highly complex secrets in my life, I want someone to listen and interact with me who knows what they are doing. Your best friend might stick with you through thick and thin. But he or she is probably not trained to be a competent counselor.

In every community in which I live, I become a client of a dentist, a family physician, an eye doctor, and an allergist. My children are placed with a good pediatrician, and my wife consults a gynecologist. But I have also learned to initiate a professional relationship with a pastoral counselor or psychologist, because from time to time I need to sit down and talk about me. And when I do, I want somebody who is as skilled, objective, and compassionate as my family physician. I have learned that this person is essential for my long-term health.

Future Directions

After we have finally divulged our long-held secrets of shame, it is important to know where to go from there. Take as an example a man who has had an extramarital affair. Now that he has confided to his pastor or therapist, should he tell anyone else, particularly his wife?

Each person and each situation is uniquely different. In some situations such confessions with a spouse might lead to a stronger marriage. In other situations it might be totally destructive. A skilled counselor can help analyze each situation.

Timing is also important. Having once verbalized our secret, we may need to be in therapy for a period of weeks before we feel ready to take a second step and share our secret with someone else. Bobby was in daily therapy for six weeks before the time was right to confide in his parents. Again, such judgment calls and questions of timing can best be handled when a person is in conversation with a trained and objective pastoral counselor or therapist. Such decisions should not be made alone.

Clearly, when we know we've got to talk to somebody about the true and full story of our lives, the first place to go is to a competent pastoral counselor or therapist. Spouses, friends, and next-door neighbors may come later. But first seek confidentiality, expertise, and trained guidance.

GOD AND THE HEALING OF SHAME

Above all, a Christian must remember that God, too, has an important role—indeed, the most important role—in the healing of our
shameful secrets. Psychology and therapy sessions alone will not do.
As the old African American spiritual states, it is God that "heals the
sin-sick soul."

Perhaps Jesus' most profound parable is a story most frequently
referred to as "The Parable of the Prodigal Son." In this parable we
hear the story of Bobby told centuries before Vietnam. A father's
youngest son seeks his independence, goes his own way, and is soon
mired in the compulsive grasp of substance abuse and sex addiction.
Finally, when his pain grows unbearable, he realizes that he must
return to his father—the symbol of God—and retch up the secrets of
his soul.

The young man expects to be rejected. He knows he will not be
understood. He imagines the worst. He will be welcomed back at
best as a slave, but never as a son. And so he returns, not able to look
his father in the eye, and offers his servitude for life.

Quite unexpectedly the father, tears of joy streaming down his
face, lifts his kneeling boy to his feet and embraces him. He puts a
family signet ring on his finger, a new robe around his thin shoulders,
shoes on his battered feet, and insists that a welcome-home party be
immediately given for his youngest son. The boy's shame is thrown
to the winds. His waywardness is dismissed. All that is important is
that "my son was lost; now he is found."

So it is with God. We cannot earn his forgiveness. It is free. We
cannot grovel in our shame. He won't allow it. God demands a party
of celebration. And Jesus insists that this is God's nature.

Speaking plainly, all that God wants from you is you. He wants
you to come home. He desires that you leave your secrets and your
shame in a far-off land and come home. God doesn't keep score. He
doesn't count sins. He is gracious and good, and his mercy endures
forever.

RESISTING THE AHAB SYNDROME

Many of us, like Captain Ahab, have been maimed and wounded by events in life that have shamed us. Indeed we are so full of shame and fear that we are compulsively driven to spend the rest of our lives seeking to harpoon that terrible truth every time it rises to the surface of our lives. But secrets kept beneath the surface will kill us. That monstrous whale will rise from the deep, flipping our fragile boat and crew members into the air and to destruction.

Again, it's better to quit chasing the whale. Give the monster his freedom. Let him rise to the surface and be seen. For it is then that we begin our pilgrimage to emotional and spiritual freedom. It is then that we return to God.

Chapter Three

RECEIVE FORGIVENESS
AND GRACE

PERHAPS THE GREATEST LESSON THAT I HAVE LEARNED from my
years of listening to people's stories is that, for all our differences, we are all much the same. Sure, we come in different shapes
and sizes. Our personalities are as unique as snowflakes and finger-
prints. And our stories are so original and varied that each person's
life reads like a new novel—too good to put down. Yet, behind the
differences in story and setting, the basic themes of our lives are so
very much alike.

We have seen some of these common themes already—the quest
for the blessing, and the struggle with secrets and shame. However,
another theme we should explore is our deep need for forgiveness.
Without a sense of forgiveness, we can never be truly free.

The quest for forgiveness is universal. Something within us
causes us to realize that we are not what we should be . . . want to be
. . . can be . . . will ever be. We desperately long to cry, "I'm sorry" and
feel not only forgiven, but accepted and free. All of this is involved in
what I call "the human situation."

THE HUMAN SITUATION

The human situation is difficult to define because it is an experiential term. The human situation is a realization that comes only from long years of living and from making many mistakes. It is a dawning awareness that we are all pretty much alike—sinner and saint, rich and poor, banker and field hand, waitress and debutante. There is within us all a common composite of themes, a similarity in battleground and struggle.

John Bradford was a Protestant minister in England during the religious warfare of the sixteenth century. When Bloody Mary came to the throne and attempted to restore Roman Catholicism as the state religion, Bradford was jailed for eighteen months and finally burned at the stake for being found guilty of heresy. During his long imprisonment, he had much time and experience to reflect on the human situation.

During those long months in jail he ate and slept with thieves, murderers, rapists, and other incorrigible criminals. He lived and talked with the bitterly poor who were jailed simply because they could not pay a debt. And he met other men like himself, men of virtue and principle, who were unwilling to forfeit religious liberty.

One day, as the jail door clanged open yet another time and some coarse criminals were dragged off screaming to their fate upon the gallows, Bradford sagged against the stone prison wall and uttered these words: "But for the grace of God, there go I."

Bradford knew that even though he was a minister and a man of principle, he was no different from nor better than the murderer swinging upon the gallows. Only circumstance and "the grace of God" had made the difference. In a prison Bradford discovered the human situation and said, "There go I."

Many times I have watched and listened carefully as emotionally stifled men and women have struggled to tell me their story. As they come to disclose the darker side of their lives, they struggle and cringe. Words fail them. Nerves falter. They feel that their condition is unique, and they are convinced that few, if any, of their respected friends could possibly have their problems, experience their feelings, commit their sins, or harbor their fantasies. Because they have not yet realized "the human situation," they feel all alone, alienated, perverted, and, yes, sinful. They are imprisoned by guilt and remorse and are not able to accept themselves.

Harry Emerson Fosdick was one of the greatest American pastors of this century. For many years he served as the senior minister of the prestigious Riverside Church in New York City. People who heard him preach in the vigor of his middle age assumed that he had always "had it all together" and had risen like cream to the top.

But as a young adult and fledgling minister, Fosdick had gone through some very difficult times. Faced with his own sensitive but hard-driving disposition, as well as the harsh demands of a parish, he had suffered a devastating nervous breakdown during his twenties. He was forced to "face the demons" within himself and often wondered whether he would ever regain his health.

Many years later, when his health was again robust and life was in balance, people flocked to Dr. Fosdick for pastoral counseling. Often men and women would enter his office determined to disclose their deepest problems but would find themselves at a loss for words, embarrassed to express their deepest feelings. At such moments Dr. Fosdick would quietly say, "Relax. Let me try to tell you how I think you are feeling." Then from the wellspring of his own struggle and experience, as well as from having listened to the stories of hundreds of others, he would begin to describe some of these people's innermost feelings. Frequently their mouths would drop open in amazement. And more with a sense of vast relief than timidity, they would exclaim, "How could you possibly know?"

How did he know? Dr Fosdick had come to recognize the complexities and nuances of the "human situation" through personal experience. Though once imprisoned by his own guilt and fears, he was now free to openly relate and empathize with others. With John Bradford he could look into the lives of most men and women and say, "There go I. . . ." Somehow Fosdick's open confession of his own struggle was the key that opened the locked prison doors for others to be liberated from guilt and shame.

The theme of "sin, grace, and forgiveness" is all wrapped up in this issue of "the human situation." For as the Apostle Paul so cogently stated, "*All* have sinned and fall short of the glory of God" (Rom. 3:23, emphasis added). Before we can really deal with our enslavement to sin and be liberated by what has been traditionally called "the grace of God," we must begin to understand the human situation. And this comes through what I call a Damascus road encounter.

THE DAMASCUS ROAD ENCOUNTER

The Apostle Paul is the New Testament writer who presents what has been traditionally called the doctrine of forgiveness and grace. There is a natural reason for this. Paul's understanding of grace and forgiveness was not an intellectual discovery. It was the result of his life being placed on the iron anvil of experience and being melted and beaten and prodded into shape. As we read his brilliant words in chapters 5 through 7 of the book of Romans, we become acutely aware that he had an intimate knowledge of sin, forgiveness, and grace and was struggling to make it clear for his readers.

As a young Jewish Pharisee, Paul was an up-and-coming young man. Many years after his conversion to Christianity he described himself this way:

> If anyone else has a mind to put confidence in the flesh, I far more: circumcised the eighth day, of the nation of Israel, of the tribe of Benjamin, a Hebrew of Hebrews, as to the Law, a Pharisee; as to zeal, a persecutor of the church, as to the righteousness which is in the Law, found blameless. . . . And I was advancing in Judaism beyond many of my contemporaries among my countrymen, being more extremely zealous for my ancestral traditions. (Phil. 3:4–6; Gal. 1:14)

Without a doubt Paul, or Saul, as he was known then, was a man to be respected. Yet an emotional war was being waged within him. The harder he tried to be righteous, the more aware he became that he was unrighteous. He had been imprisoned by an abundance of guilt that led to legalistic compulsive behavior and a murderous hatred of Christians.

But one day he had a dramatic meeting on the road from Jerusalem to Damascus. The fiery Pharisee and his party were going to Damascus to arrest some Christians and bring them back for trial in Jerusalem. Suddenly their progress was interrupted. As Paul later described the scene, "A very bright light suddenly flashed from heaven all around me, and I, fell to the ground and heard a voice saying to me, 'Saul, Saul, why are you persecuting me?' And I answered, 'Who are Thou, Lord?' And He said to me, 'I am Jesus the Nazarene, whom you are persecuting'" (Acts 22:6-8).

What exactly happened on the Damascus road? We don't fully know, but Paul was convinced beyond a doubt that he had met Jesus of Nazareth and that he was the Messiah. I believe that through this encounter Paul became aware of a deep spiritual truth, which he was later to call "grace."

Why do I believe this? Simply because of the radical change in Paul's life. Not only did he come to believe that Jesus was the promised Messiah, but he also came to view very differently the Hebrew Law, which he had scrupulously committed his whole life to keeping and defending.

Before his Damascus road experience, Paul firmly believed that keeping the thousands of Jewish laws was what made him righteous and acceptable to God. Yet, inwardly, Paul knew the true situation. He knew the lust and covetousness and pride that boiled within him. He was aware of the envy and hatred and jealousy he struggled to repress. He realized that human blood was on his hands. And the more he tried to be "good," the more he was convinced he was "bad."

On the Damascus road, Paul was finally knocked off his high horse of legalism and righteousness and fell flat on his back. Exposed in the brilliance of a heavenly light, he knew God could see right through him. But in that bright light there was also a loving warmth. And out of that warmth Paul received a freeing message. It was as if God was saying, "Paul, you can be no better than you presently are. But sins and all, I accept you for who you are. Don't let your guilt imprison you. Now, get up! You are free to be your true self and to love others as I love you."

It was out of that experience that Paul coined the word *grace,* which he used prolifically in his preaching and writing. In cryptic language that is hard for us to follow, Paul explains it to the Christians in Rome:

> For sin shall not be master over you, for you are not under Law, but under grace. What then? Shall we sin because we are not under Law but under grace? May it never be! . . . But now having been freed from sin and enslaved to God, you derive your benefit, resulting in sanctification and the outcome, eternal life. For the wages of sin is death, but the free gift of God is eternal life in Christ Jesus our Lord. (Rom. 6:14-15, 22-23)

Paul's message of grace boiled down to this: "Try as you might, you cannot be righteous. But God accepts you as you are. And God's acceptance can free you to be less controlled by sin and guilt and more motivated by love."

On the Damascus road Paul had to accept the fact he could not rise above the human situation. But, surprise of all surprises, he discovered that God loved him anyway and wanted to live in relationship with him. Paul was now free to accept himself, warts and all.

THE GRACE EXPERIENCE

I do not personally know anyone who has been literally blinded by a great light and knocked to his knees, but I have heard the stories of many people who have been slammed by life into encountering the grace experience. One of these people is a young man named Tim.

Tim, like Paul, grew up exemplary in every way. He was a brilliant student, an exceptional athlete, and a popular fellow. He had a very natural theological curiosity and a deep reverence for God. Raised in an ultraconservative Protestant family in America's Bible Belt, he attended church from infancy. Never smug or pious, however, he was a loving "good old boy" who was fun to be around.

During his adolescent years Tim continued to be active in his church. He was involved in mission projects and youth choir, and he was a leader in his youth group. But, as with most teenagers, he sometimes felt rebellious; the wonder and passion of his own sexuality was demanding expression. For the first time Tim began to struggle with the question of sin and grace.

Tim had never really struggled with sin. Other than telling a few lies in early childhood (for which he was severely punished), and throwing a few dirt clods at passing cars (for which he was never caught), Tim had lived a calm life. He was a good kid.

When Tim was four years old he was caught playing doctor with the little girl next door, both naked as jaybirds. His mother, to put it mildly, was not the least bit amused. From that moment on he knew that the secrets of the opposite sex were strictly taboo—not to be touched, explored, or talked about.

When Tim was sixteen, however, a true emotional war began to rage. Sexuality seldom had been discussed in Tim's home. From what he could see of his parents, he was sure he had been conceived through an affectionate kiss bestowed by his father every evening on his mother's forehead, and certainly nothing more.

Now as a big, muscular sixteen-year-old with natural good looks, Tim was a constant subject of conversation among the girls. Beneath his athletic virility Tim was shy and somewhat reserved, but he enjoyed his popularity and attractiveness.

During his junior year of high school, it finally happened. Tim fell head over heels for a petite cheerleader named Jan. His reserve melted away and the infatuation of a lifetime began. Tim and Jan were good kids and good for each other.

Tim and Jan had been brought up with the belief that premarital sex was wrong. Not only were they taught this at home, but they claimed to believe it themselves. But they were very human teenagers, and sexuality was very real. Over time their relationship became more and more physical. One day Tim came home to find that his mother had suggestively left a book on his bed. It was entitled, *What Every Boy Should Know.* In scanning the book, Tim discovered that he and Jan were engaged in "heavy petting." He'd always called it "making out."

Heavy petting or not, Tim was a person of principle and took his Christian faith seriously. He had determined not to experience sexual intercourse before marriage. And even though he was sure from locker-room talk that many of his friends were sexually active, he did not weaken in his resolve.

However, guilt was building deep within Tim. From early adolescence he had been hounded by the very natural drive to masturbate, and it became his secret shame.[1] Now, fueled with a growing sexual drive, he was sure something was wrong with him. Not aware that masturbation is a normal activity of adolescence he began to believe that he was oversexed, even perverted. He became imprisoned and isolated by his guilt- and shame-induced secrecy.

As Tim and Jan's relationship continued on through their senior year, they suddenly reached a plateau. They sensed they could not go further relationally or sexually without a deeper, more binding commitment to one another. Even though they talked of marriage, they realized it would be years away. Tim was being recruited by several colleges to play football. Jan wanted to fulfill her dream of being a nurse. And so their relationship slid into neutral.

When college and nursing school finally became reality, Tim and Jan gradually experienced a distancing in their relationship. They began to date other people, and slowly their thoughts of marriage to each other dissolved.

Tim enjoyed his newfound independence and soon began to date other girls. And even though he didn't develop a steady relationship as he had in high school, he did have some short-lived and intense dating experiences. He was reaching the years of his greatest sexual prowess, and his blood ran as hot as his fantasies.

Even though he had never gone to bed with a girl or shared in sexual intercourse, he began to fear that he was obsessed with sexual thoughts. He also felt that he was "bad," a little out of healthy balance, "an accident waiting to happen." His own feelings of shame drove him further into secrecy. Yet, on the surface, Tim was a model, all–American kid—a college football player, a good student, an out-going Christian, and a fun person to be around.

Perhaps Tim seems a little neurotic—someone who is hung up by sexual repression and inordinate guilt. But I suspect that most of us can identify with his struggle. Perhaps the craziest thing of all is that even though Tim was one of the few young men his age who had not had sex, he felt as guilty as if he were the most promiscuous person on campus. Guilt—deserved and undeserved—often rages in the hearts of the most exemplary of people. And it prevents us from finding contentment.

During his senior year in college, Tim met a transfer student named Carol and fell head over heels in love. By Christmas they were engaged, and four days after June graduation they were married. Lying in the midst of honeymoon bliss, Tim felt a sense of relief and subtle pride. Somehow he had been true to this one girl. And even though he didn't feel haughty or judgmental toward others, he was glad that he had kept a commitment to himself.

Tim and Carol soon moved to another state, where Tim would attend law school. After renting a small apartment, they adjusted well to a new life together.

However, Tim soon discovered there was one thing he hadn't left behind—his old sense of guilt. Even though he was totally faithful to Carol, he discovered that marriage did not "strike him blind." Other girls still remained beautiful and attractive. And though he was not flirtatious, he sometimes found himself attracted to them. "If I were single, I'd sure date her," he would sometimes say in silence. Slowly a fear began to emerge. Often he would think, "If I don't watch it, I'll mess up and have an affair." And the more he tried to repress these thoughts, the more he dwelled upon them. A young man who had never been unfaithful—who had had sex with only the woman he married—was hounded by fears of having an affair.

Tim kept all of these thoughts to himself. He certainly couldn't tell Carol. And who else would understand? He was sure his minister would be appalled, and he was too embarrassed to tell a friend. So for months and years he sat on a fear that would rise up only to be shoved back down again.

Several years after law school Tim finally had his Damascus road experience. One day a beautiful young woman came to Tim's law office. A year earlier, her husband had left her for another woman, and now divorce proceedings were beginning. She asked Tim to represent her.

As she poured out her story, Tim began to feel a deep empathy for this hurting woman. And she saw in Tim a strong, supportive, and sympathetic person. They both began to feel a natural attraction for one another that quickly moved into infatuation.

Tim was not completely naive; his domestic-law professor had spoken very frankly about such situations. Tim knew that his client was emotionally vulnerable. He also sensed that she was willing to have an affair. And yet, try as he might, he couldn't objectively and professionally confront a snowballing situation. He avoided telling her that they needed either to realize what was happening and change course, or terminate their professional relationship.

Tim later said, "I felt like I did as a kid when one afternoon I picked up an electric saw that was not grounded. It had a short and almost electrocuted me. Try as I might, I could not let go of the steel handle. It was welded to my hand. Had my dad not pulled the plug out of the socket, I guess it would have killed me."

What was keeping Tim from letting go of the electric infatuation with his client was not passion and lust as much as it was guilt and fear. In Tim's lifelong quest to be faithful to his convictions, he had heaped up mountains of guilt and a fear of "messing up." And now he couldn't "let go of the saw." The high voltage of guilt was paralyzing him. For it is often guilt that keeps us in bondage just as much as sin.

One day his client came for a four o'clock appointment. As Tim busily took notes, discussed options, and reviewed her case, he lost all track of time. Finally he looked down at his watch. It was after five. The secretaries left at five and his partner was out of town. They were alone.

She knew it too. In fact Tim suddenly suspected that she had prolonged their meeting, knowing that everyone left the office at five. There was something about her look and inviting smile that told him the ball was in his court. The choice was his. His heart raced and his hands grew clammy.

Keeping his eyes on his papers, he signed the last document and stood up. "Well, I'll see you in court on Monday at ten o'clock," he said. "Yeah," she softly replied, "I guess so." Walking around the desk and gazing out a window, Tim noticed that in the height of winter it was already dark. He took her coat from the coat rack and held it out for her to put on. As she turned her back to him, placing her arms in the coat sleeves, she seemed so openly vulnerable. He felt as if he were embracing her. And then turning, her fur collar softening her face, she suddenly embraced him and said, "Thanks so much, Tim. You don't know how much help you've been."

Tim knew the moment had come. Slowly she lifted her face up to him and Tim released her. Turning to pick up a folder from his desk, he muttered, "I'll see you to the door." From his voice inflection, he sounded gullible and naive. But inside his heart was pounding. He had come within a fraction of an inch of making a major mistake, and he knew it.

Scarcely a minute later, he walked back into his office. He locked his office door, turned off the lights, and sagged down in a chair in the darkness. With all his soul he wanted to cry, to wash away all of the guilt and fear and repression and lust. And then he heard a voice say, "Oh God, I give up! I'm no good! I'm just no damn good!" It was his voice. His breaking voice. And he doubled up, sobbing.

The next morning Tim nervously called his pastor. He made an appointment to see him late that afternoon. Like a man being led to the guillotine, he drove to the church. Slowly, over the course of several weeks, he poured out the story of his guilt over masturbation, of his teenage sexual struggle with Jan, of his growing obsessive fear of having an affair, and of the recent event with his client.

Fortunately for Tim, his pastor was trained and skilled in counseling. In the weeks that followed, Tim came to understand why he had been so captivated and controlled by guilt. And yet the greatest healing did not take place through counseling. Rather, understanding took place through counseling. But Tim was released from bondage on that dark night of surrender—the Damascus road encounter—in his office.

As Tim later said, "When I heard my voice say, 'I give up! I'm just no damn good!' it was like the time my father jerked the plug from the wall socket and I could at last let go of that electric saw that was killing me. For years I had wanted with all my heart to let go. But until I finally realized that I—Tim—was a weak human being and probably wouldn't get better, I couldn't let go. And when I did, in the darkness of that night, I somehow knew that God loved me and accepted me, just as I was. I was the prodigal son come home."

This story may seem a bit overblown, but I believe it reflects the human situation. And it gives us insight into what the Apostle Paul meant when he wrote about grace.

Most Christians try very hard to live an upright and righteous life. We try to match our actions with our words. Tim certainly did in his determination not to become involved with sex before marriage. But underneath it all he knew what Jesus meant when he said, "You have heard that it was said, 'You shall not commit adultery'; but I say to you, that everyone who looks on a woman to lust for her has committed adultery already with her in his heart" (Matt 5:27-28). In these words of Jesus we have a vivid picture of the human situation. Inwardly, outwardly, no matter how hard we try—we are all guilty of being sinners. And until we honestly confront that truth, we cannot let go of that deathly electric current of moral destruction. Guilt controls our life.

In our struggle for personal freedom it is essential to understand that we cannot be freed from the compulsive, sin-inducing guilt of our life until we realize that we are no better than anyone else. Only then can we relax our attempts to be righteous and admit as John Bradford did as he looked around him in jail, "There go I!" It takes a lot of living and a lot of struggle to reach this point.

Yet Bradford said more than "There go I." He said, "But for the grace of God, there go I." Because Bradford had accepted the reality of the human situation, he had been freed to let go of the destructive behavior that would have led him to the spiritual gallows. This knowledge that he was a sinner but God loved him anyway had released him from guilt—from compulsive behavior—to be more like Christ. Grace had saved him from self-destruction.

Admittedly, when Paul preached his gospel of grace, many heard it and said in so many words, "Well, if we're freed from the Law . . . if we're all sinners and God loves us anyway . . . let's just keep on sinning and enjoy it." But to think that way is to completely misunderstand the grace of God. The experience of grace sets us free to be our truest selves. Like the healed demoniac, we become clothed and in our right mind (Mark 5:15). And though we are still sinful people, we are no longer controlled by sin.

It has frequently been suggested that the three greatest interpreters of the Christian faith are the Apostle Paul, Augustine of Hippo, and Martin Luther. Though living in different centuries and cultures, these men shared one thing in common. They each were relentlessly driven to a point in their adult life where they became appalled and defeated by their sinfulness. And each of them gave up on their ability to be better. As a result they were thrust helplessly upon the grace of God. This experience opened their eyes to see the heart of the gospel and caused them to focus their teaching on the doctrine of grace.

Granted, grace remained a perplexing mystery for these great theologians. That is why Augustine humbly confessed, "What is grace? I know until you ask me; when you ask me, I do not know."[2] Grace defies our reason. It jumbles our words. It skews our logic and remains an enigma. Yet these three great Christian thinkers have dredged the depths of spiritual truth and know that grace alone can free us from our sins. And grace alone can help us overcome the destructive drivenness in our lives.

Perhaps the following incident best illustrates the wonder of God's forgiveness and grace in response to the compulsive drivenness induced by guilt. I was once on a church retreat with some college students at the beach. I was relaxing in a rocking chair on a wide front porch facing the Atlantic Ocean when I was jarred from my daydreaming by the alarmed screams of some of the kids on the beach.

When I dashed down to the water's edge I could see three of our boys swimming about fifty yards away. They were obviously in trouble. A riptide had seized them and was towing them further and further out to sea. I was paralyzed with fear and helplessness and knew there was little we on the beach could do.

Fortunately one of the struggling boys was an experienced swimmer and understood the ways of the ocean. He instructed his friends to quit fighting the current and float. He knew that if they fought the riptide, they would become exhausted and drown. On the other hand, if they relaxed and floated, sooner or later they would drift free of the mighty grip of the current and could then swim back to the safety of the shore. This is exactly what happened. A mile or so down the beach the riptide lost its force, and they were able to swim to shore.

Guilt is the dangerous riptide of our lives, the devil's favorite device. Guilt catches us in its malignant and powerful grasp and as long as we fight it, it will not let us go. However, when we quit fighting and begin to float in the forgiveness and grace of God, we are strangely released from bondage and set free to return to safety.

Remember the words of Paul to the Galatian Christians: "It was for freedom that Christ set us free; therefore keep standing firm and do not be subject again to the yoke of slavery" (Gal. 5:1).

Chapter Four

CONFRONT DEADLY SCRIPTS

R OBERT WAS AN UNUSUALLY SUCCESSFUL YOUNG MAN. Now in his mid-thirties, he had climbed quickly to the top of his pro-fessional mountain. He was a realtor whose name was prominently seen on the "For Sale" signs in the yard of almost every vacant house in the county. In the fifteen short years following his college graduation, Robert had amassed a small fortune and seemed to be set for life.

Recently he had considered throwing his hat into the political ring. One of the local state legislators was retiring and it was an opportune time to run for office. His realty company was now so well-tuned that it could run smoothly without his daily presence. Perhaps it was time to broaden his horizons and start a second career.

I first met Robert when he came to me for counseling. For sev-eral months he had been experiencing mild but persistent depression. Lately the depression had been building in intensity. Normally a happy-go-lucky person, he was now frightened by his depression. His physician found him to be in good physical condition and suggested that he spend some time talking with a pastor or a psychotherapist. He came to see me.

As we talked, it became apparent that much of his depression was centered on his indecision about running for political office. On the surface it seemed to be a fairly simple and straightforward decision. He clearly wanted to enter the race. Professionally and financially he could afford the challenge, and he had his family's support and blessing. But something still caused Robert to vacillate.

One day as we talked, I said, "If you can't get internal permission to run for office, why don't you just sit out this election and wait until later? There will be other opportunities."

Almost without thinking Robert shot back, "I don't have time to lose. It's probably now or never."

When I asked him what he meant by his remark, he grew silent. Finally he said in an embarrassed voice, "I don't think I'll live to be an old man. I'll probably die young. And if I'm going to run for office, I'd better do it now."

I knew intuitively that a trump card had just been laid upon the table. The rapid success of Robert's life, the intense drivenness of his personality, and his present struggle with depression were all tied up in his belief that he would probably die young. He felt that his clock was running down.

Robert admitted that he had never told his wife or anyone else that he feared an early death. To do so would embarrass him and make him feel silly. It was just a veiled apprehension he had lived with since childhood. Smoldering in the secrecy of his own mind, the fear of early death had relentlessly pushed this young stallion to come out of the starting gates fast and fly to the head of the pack. His life had been lived at breakneck speed and now the political race would accelerate it further. Could he stand the pace? Could he justify his reasons? Faced with these questions, and feeling helplessly out of control, he had certainly been a prime candidate for depression.

I am amazed at how many older adults tell me that in their young adult years they feared an early death. Recently a close friend described how he threw an extravagant party on his fiftieth birthday because he had been convinced for most of his adult life that he would never live to be fifty. Now, at the relaxed age of sixty-five, he feels that his last fifteen years have been his best and most productive.

Yes, I am amazed at how many people share my friend's problem. But I'm not amazed that people experience fear of early death, for I have also had to wrestle with this phenomenon.

THE SCRIPT

Somewhere in my childhood I came to believe that it was a trait of male members of my family to die young. Nobody ever told me this. I simply assumed it.

Both of my grandfathers died before I was born—one from a head injury received in a fall, and the other of infection from a perforated stomach ulcer. In our family only grandmothers had gray hair.

My father didn't help the situation. When I was a child he told me on several occasions what to do, "should I not be around and you need to take care of your mother." I soon got the picture. He feared that he would die young, like his father.

Ironically, he did. When I was fourteen and he was forty-six, Dad died of a heart attack. This intergenerational repetition of early death was eerie. Even a young and active teenager could not be oblivious to it.

I don't remember losing sleep over this at the time. After all, a forty-six-year-old father is remarkably ancient in the eyes of a young teenager. However, when I was a seminary student in my twenties, the idea of dying young surfaced ominously.

I remember the day well. I was listening to a lecture on career ministry. The professor was talking about the developmental issues that face a minister over the long span of his or her career. Suddenly I realized that I had never pictured turning fifty. Neither had I given a thought to retirement. I was shocked! I had never consciously said, "Scott, you will die young." But I suddenly realized that I was living my life and projecting my future as if life would automatically stop before I reached fifty. I left the classroom that day a little dazed and shaken. I knew this was an attitude I needed to confront.

As I explored this subject with a pastoral counselor, I discovered a term called *life-scripts* or simply, *scripts.*[1] A script is a life plan, very much like a dramatic stage script, which we often subconsciously feel compelled to fulfill. Like an actor or actress on life's stage, we play the part and enact the scenes the script dictates. Such a script is usually created and integrated into our mind and perception as the result of childhood transactions with our parents. It then becomes a road map to follow on the journey of life.

Many destructive scripts do not deal with death issues. A host of other debilitating themes can also be scripted. For instance, Lewis is the eldest son of a very successful lawyer. He knew it was assumed he, too, would be a lawyer. His parents strongly intimated that the family law practice "will one day be yours." And even his friends acted as if his future was preordained.

In his teenage years, when it became clear that Lewis had unique artistic talents, he gave serious thought to becoming an architect. Yet, even though he wanted passionately to be an architect, he felt that he would betray "something down deep"—his life-script—if he did. So he went to law school, became a lawyer, and is now in frequent tension with his profession. He is faithfully living out a script—at great personal cost—of a life plan he did not write but merely accepted.

Ann is the second of three children. Though deeply loved, she was always described as simply "cute," and was never encouraged to excel. In contrast, her parents were convinced that her older brother, Tom, was a child prodigy. They pictured him growing up and discovering a cure for cancer or being the next Einstein. And Ann's younger sister, Ellen, was unusually pretty. Very early, Ellen's talents had been polished for appearances in beauty contests. She was pushed by her mother to excel at piano and dance. In the middle of all this, Ann remained "good, sweet, cute Ann."

In reality Ann has equal intelligence with her brother and more innate talent than her sister. But now, as a sophomore in college, she is a C+ student and is still being cute and likable. To do otherwise would threaten her script and cause emotional—if not relational—disequilibrium. Until she recognizes her script and intentionally alters it, she will tend to stay in the middle of the pack.

Dale is an immensely talented and intelligent fellow. However, he is being greatly influenced by a failure script—to the extent that his life is being jeopardized. Dale's grandfather was a cattle rancher who had been wiped out by the Great Depression. One brutal winter in 1931 he had to shoot hundreds of his cattle to keep them from starving to death. He never bounced back. He became a bitter man and slid into alcoholism.

Dale's father left the ranch and moved to the city. An industrious businessman, he attempted to make up for the past and establish an empire. Several times it seemed that he had all the dominoes lined up just right. Then one would fall and all the rest toppled over. After three declarations of bankruptcy, he bought a small but stable dry-cleaning business and now muses over how things might have been.

Dale is thirty. He, too, is a businessman and has done quite well. Yet he lives as if a black cloud hangs over his head. Several times he has been aware that he has unwittingly almost sabotaged important business deals. He realizes that he has an inordinate fear of failure and has to consciously fight against the feeling that "no matter what I do, at some point I am going to fail." Such internal pressure has prodded him to drink hard on weekends, and he finds himself reflecting, in unguarded moments, upon his grandfather.

Many of us have become slaves to the destructive scripts in our lives and are trying desperately to live out these scripts—much to our own detriment. As a rule, we are not aware of doing this. But somewhere in our subconscious past Mother implied, "You are like this," or Daddy suggested, "Your life will be this way," and we have naively accepted their direction for our lives. In doing so we have truly lost our freedom to be our authentic selves.

There are two dangers to scripts. First, they forbid us to direct our own lives. We end up struggling to live out someone else's dreams, opinions, beliefs, or thinking and not our own. Second, the scripts are often destructive. They cause us to inflict enormous emotional stress on ourselves and frequently limit our growth and self-fulfillment.

One of the most destructive and common life-scripts is the "I'll die young" script. If we do not recognize and deal with this script, it has a tragic tendency to become reality. Let us look further at this particular script, because it gives insight into the nature of various forms of destructive scripts.

TIME COMPRESSION

I do not believe in determinism as such. Just because we anticipate or fear something does not mean that it is going to happen. My sixty-five-year-old friend who thought he would die before reaching age fifty obviously did not. However, having said this, we must see that the "I'll die young" script certainly doesn't aid or enhance our emotional health or contribute to long life.

One of the major effects of the "I'll die young" script is that it often causes a phenomenon I call time compression. Since we feel we must live all of our life and accomplish all of our dreams in half the time as others, we compress time and try to do everything in double time. As a result we become driven people—slaves to negative thoughts and vague feelings of anxiety.

Robert, the young realtor, is a perfect example of a man caught in time compression. He put it this way: "If I'm going to do it, I'd better do it now." This young man had a pervading sense that time was running out, and so he spurred himself to beat the clock. He would squeeze it all in somehow. He rationalized his drivenness by saying, "Well, what the heck! I'd rather burn out than rust out, anyway."

I firmly believe that burning out and rusting out are not the best or only options for living our lives. We all need to use and perfect the abilities God has given us. I greatly respect achievement, ambition, and success. But a compulsive sense of time compression can prematurely destroy a life that has only been partly actualized. And that is a supreme waste and a tragedy.

How can time compression lead to the deterioration of health and possibly to death? In recent years medical research has demonstrated that a heightened sense of urgency over an extended period leads to biochemical and physiological changes that often result in cardiovascular disease. Dr. Meyer Friedman and Dr. Ray Rosenman have particularly popularized this medical finding in their research and writing on Type A behavior.[2] Continued research is validating their findings.

The conscious and subconscious pressures of living under such an incessant state of drivenness can result in a host of other stress-induced or stress-aggravated ailments such as stomach ulcers, colitis, arthritis, and migraine headaches. There is no doubt that a prolonged sense of time urgency or time compression has an adverse affect on our health. As a result the "I'll die young" script can become a self-fulfilling prophecy.

Perhaps the greatest damage inflicted by living in a state of time compression is that we do not enjoy and savor the present moment—the life that is ours to live now. Racing to beat the clock, our sixteen-hour work days make us numb to the beauty and enjoyment of life. Life becomes like eating candy with the wrapper still on it or taking a hot shower while wearing a raincoat. We cannot relax long enough, stand still long enough, or adequately idle our engines to enjoy the flavor and the warmth of life around us. Instead we must hurry on to achieve another success or accept another challenge.

REWRITING YOUR SCRIPT

What can you do if you realize that somewhere in your past you bought into the "I'll die young" script—or any other form of scripted living—and you are leading an exhaustingly driven life? First, I should say that there is no one thing that will significantly alter your script. But there are a combination of things you can do that will make it possible to rewrite your own script.

Recognition

As with so many personal problems, the first step toward a remedy and freedom is the not-so-simple task of recognition. To solve a problem we first have to admit that we have a problem. And to recognize that we have been following a destructive script requires a lot of courage.

Most of us don't talk much about dying. To think about death at all takes some deliberate discipline. As a result, many people resist updating their wills or reviewing their life insurance policies until a few days before they are scheduled for major surgery or shortly before leaving on an extensive trip. Since none of us want to think about our own death, our "I'll die young" scripts often remain submerged and unrecognized, silently haunting us as we go about our day-to-day routines.

How can we recognize an "I'll die young" script? Let's try asking ourselves these questions:

1. Do I feel an urgent need to accomplish my major ambition by the time I am forty-five or fifty? If so, why?

2. Am I saving money for my children's college education? Can I see myself participating in my children's weddings? Can I picture myself playing with my grandchildren?

3. Do I sometimes find myself thinking about what personal possessions I want to pass on to my children or friends when I die? How old will the recipients be?

4. What are my fantasies about retirement? Do I have some definite dreams and ambitions? Or am I having difficulty visualizing retirement?

5. Do I frequently wonder if my spouse will remarry when I die? If so, what will my spouse look like? Do I imagine him or her as young, middle-aged, or old?

6. Am I overly concerned with life insurance? Do I refuse to think about it at all?

Perhaps our answers to these six simple questions will help us see whether we have the freedom to picture ourselves living a good long life, or whether we have become slaves to the obsession that we will die young.

But there is good news: If we've been flirting with the "I'll die young" script—or any other scripts—we can rewrite the script. We can slow down that clock and remove ourselves from time compression and its ill effects. But to accomplish that and become free once and for all from the "I'll die young" script, we've got to recognize it for what it is.

Exposure

Once we've recognized a destructive script for what it is, the next step toward rewriting it and moving toward freedom is to expose the script. We must open up and talk about it. Once we begin to expose negative scripts to fresh air and daylight—to tell somebody else about them—we are on the way to changing our destructive behavior and altering our script.

Recently a respected pastor-friend of mine realized that he was not spending enough time with his family. The demands of his church were causing him to neglect the needs of his wife and children. In the privacy of his soul he resolved to do something about this, and yet nothing changed. Months went by and still he was not spending any more time with his family. He despaired of ever being able to alter his lifestyle.

Finally, on the anniversary Sunday of his seventh year as pastor of his church, he decided to do something bold and different. His wife had recently undergone major surgery, and in his sermon he shared with the congregation some lessons he had learned from her medical crisis. At one point in his sermon, he said, "Not the least of the lessons has been a new awareness of how little I have been doing to keep the family going and how much my wife has done. There are changes overdue in that direction. You will be seeing a bit less of me so my family will see me more. Some vows need to be made public to better ensure their keeping."[3]

To make a statement like that takes courage. But it was a word warmly received by a congregation that loved him. Of course, the point is that often our silent vows do need to be shared with others to "better ensure their keeping."

I can remember how I felt several years ago, when I first began to admit to a few close friends that I was wrestling with the "I'll die young" script. I was embarrassed to expose my feelings because I was afraid they would think I was neurotic and morbid. Yet, when I did gather my courage and began to mumble a few "confessions," I found that my friends easily understood. A few of them even admitted that they struggled with this same fear.

Perhaps the person that it was hardest to talk with about this anxiety was my family doctor. One day, after receiving my annual physical, which included a treadmill stress test, I sheepishly told him that I had always feared having a heart attack like my father. He smiled, and with a wisdom that came from seeing hundreds of patients, he said, "Well, I can understand that. Something would be wrong if you didn't!" Somehow he allowed me to see that a certain amount of anxiety was normal. But I also found that talking with him openly about my concern freed me to release the fear within and to begin to write a more healthy script for my life.

Industriousness or Drivenness?

Another major step toward erasing destructive scripts is to clearly recognize the difference between creative industriousness and out-of-control drivenness.

To be an industrious person is to be someone who is hard-working and disciplined. An industrious person has a clear sense of goal orientation and strives very hard to meet those goals. Productivity is the hallmark of a conscientious and industrious person.

Management studies reveal that the most effective and productive business executives—the men and women who make up the top management of major corporations—are also industrious people who know how to control their lives. They take a day off every week, and only rarely will they take work home with them. They enjoy regular vacations and set aside time for their family. They develop recreational skills and enjoy avocational pursuits. Though industrious, hardworking, and productive, these executives control and manage their lives as efficiently as they control their business.

A driven person, in contrast, is one whose foot is constantly glued to the accelerator. Driven people cannot slow down. They work slavishly twelve and fourteen hours a day and at least six days a week. They rarely take a vacation, and when they do, they feel guilty. Even when they are at home, their minds are at work. Their lives are a mixed bag of frantic activity and they are out of control. It is as if they are being constantly pushed and prodded by an invisible and unrelenting force. Such compulsive people are chronically fatigued and seem to always be huffing and puffing up endless stairs.

A driven person must come to recognize and expose the force that is compelling him or her. Sometimes it is the "I'll die young" script. When this demon of the fear of death is cast out, then a conscious effort must be made to change one's lifestyle. Instead of being pushed and out of control, we must become industrious but in control. We'll take days off and enjoy them; we'll plan time with our families and develop relaxing avocations and hobbies. Slowly, the childlike joy of life will return and the tyranny of drivenness will be removed. We are then free to be ourselves.

There is an interesting story told in the Gospel of Luke. Jesus cast an unclean spirit out of a man. He warned that if that spirit returned and found "the house" of the healed man empty and vacant, he would then invade the man's house again along with "seven other spirits more evil than itself . . . and the last state of that man becomes worse than the first" (Luke 11:24-26).

Jesus is saying that when something bad is removed from our lives, we had better fill the resulting empty space with something good, or else the evil—or a worse evil—will return. So it is with destructive life-scripts. When we recognize a negative script, give it a name, expose it to light, and cast it out, we had better fill the vacuum with good habits. If we do not take full charge of our lives and become in control, the demon of drivenness will return and plague us again.

Good Health Habits

Driven men and women frequently have poor health habits. Besides being constantly plagued by stress that contributes to disease, they do not take the time to maintain good health.

In recent years, exercise, diet, and leisure activities have been shown to be major contributors toward good physical health. Yet a driven person who is constantly in a hurry does not take time to exercise regularly, is prone to eat junk food, and will usually postpone that golf game or tennis match to another day.

Similarly, when it comes to spiritual health, the essential disciplines of Bible study and prayer are also found to require too much time. While giving lip service to their importance, the driven person will mumble prayers while brushing his teeth and read the Bible late at night while drifting off to sleep. Thirty minutes of quiet time each day for Bible study and prayer is a demand too great for the driven person.

Yet the one thing that could greatly aid the positive alteration of an "I'll die young" script is for a person to constructively do everything possible to enrich and prolong life. There is nothing that makes us feel more in control of our lives than to regularly engage in physical exercise, spiritual discipline, and to follow wise dietary habits. While this cannot guarantee long life, it can free us to say, "I'm giving life my best shot! If I do die young, it won't be because I self-destructed."

Relate to Senior Adults

I didn't have many senior adult role models in my family. I missed knowing my grandparents, and consequently I did not relate to people as they grew older. However, when I graduated from seminary and joined the ministerial staff of the First Baptist Church of Athens, Georgia, one of my first assignments was to begin a ministry program for senior adults.

One autumn day twenty representatives of "The Graying of America" met for lunch and our senior adult ministry was launched.

Over the next few years we devoured buckets of fried chicken, logged hundreds of miles on tour buses, watched leaves turn gold in North Carolina, and swapped stories too rich ever to be forgotten. I learned to love those folks, and they gave me insight into a quality and spirit and pace of life I had never known.

I remember Reese Dunson and Ralph Tolbert. In their retirement years they tilled and planted and coddled a vegetable garden together. Once too busy with children, vocations, and responsibility to turn good earth with a hoe and spade, they now reveled in their hours together, talking and working.

Then there was Archie Langley. He loved nothing better than his University of Georgia Bulldogs. On spring afternoons he would sit in the bleachers and listen to the crack of baseball bats. On winter evenings he would hurriedly leave at the close of prayer meeting to catch the last half of the basketball games. He could always keep me updated with the latest scores and standings.

These were all good and industrious men who had given much to life. And now they were enjoying retirement years. Sure, they moved slowly and sometimes complained of aches and pains. But life was rich for them, and they lived it to the fullest.

Slowly I began to wonder if I, too, would grow old. I began to visualize a small wooded farm I wanted to own. Maybe if Beth and I could save enough, we'd be able to build that house we'd dreamed of when the kids graduated from college. And like old Archie, I'd watch every Georgia football game that was played. I don't think I'd like to garden, but I would want to be close to a library. And I'd attend every literature and history course that interested me and never worry about grades or degrees. It began to dawn on me that I'd make a pretty neat old man.

Slowly, almost imperceptibly, my life-script began to change. These "old people" suddenly made me want to grow old as well. They helped me to see that life might be longer than I had ever imagined, fuller and more enjoyable than I ever dreamed. I began to say, "I'm not going to die young! I'm going to collect my Social Security, too! And I'm going to make some other bright-eyed young minister feed me fried chicken and take me on trips and listen to all my long stories and gems of wisdom."

If you want to begin to alter your "I'll die young" script, get around some senior adults who truly enjoy life. You'll slowly discover that growing old is something worth striving for. And deep within, your horizon of life will grow broader.

Make Future Plans

You can know that you are altering your "I'll die young" script when you feel the freedom to make specific plans for your retirement years. I can dream about that farm I want; but until I begin to put money in a retirement plan while still in midlife, I am not really serious about making that dream come true.

Of course, we must live firmly rooted in the present moment. But not to prepare for the future is either foolhardy or an admission that we don't really believe we will grow old. You can be certain your "I'll die young" script is being rewritten when you get serious about planning for the future. That kind of planning doesn't mean you lack faith in God's provision for you. Rather, it is a sign of faith that God will continue to lead you and that surely goodness and mercy will follow you all the days of your life.

TALK TRUTHFULLY WITH GOD

Our own emotional honesty and strong resolve will go a long way in reshaping or removing destructive scripts from our lives. However, I have learned that it is the strength of God found through prayer and meditation that ultimately leads me to freedom.

Whenever I uncover a negative script overshadowing my life and usurping my energy, I force myself to talk with God about this script as honestly as I can. Often it is difficult to put my feelings into words. Frequently, I take a sheet of paper and struggle to write a letter to

God. Sometimes I simply sit in God's presence and am silent. But regardless of the form of communication I use to address God, it is crucial that I share my deepest struggles with him.

As I write these words I am fifty years old. I now look with eagerness toward many more years of meaningful life. I have largely lost my fear of dying young—as well as a host of other negative scripts I picked up along life's way. I can now realize that above all, it has been the strength and gentle grace of God that has enabled me to let go of such scripts and find a deeper level of contentment in my life. I could not find this freedom on my own. It was a path that God and I had to walk down together. And the long hours that I have spent talking honestly with God have been the greatest help in finding personal freedom.

Don't attempt to overcome or reshape a destructive script by yourself. You are not strong enough. But God and you can together rewrite the scripts of your life and find a level of peace and contentment you have never known.

ALL THE WORLD'S A STAGE

As I've been writing and thinking about scripts, an old memory has pushed its way to the surface. For several years during college I was a drama major. I loved to act. Acting was a passion, and through that experience I first came to understand the power of scripts.

A good actor or actress knows that he or she must become so immersed in the character being played that any other identity fades away. I, too, learned to embody my cast character for those few brief hours on stage.

I once played the part of Paul in Neil Simon's play *Barefoot in the Park,* and I soon realized a strange thing was happening. For weeks after the play was over, whenever someone would call "Paul!" I would turn around and respond as if they were talking to me. It was a little spooky. But it was a vivid illustration of the power of scripts to consume our lives.

"All the world's a stage, and all the men and women merely play-ers,"[4] said Shakespeare. If this is true, we must choose our scripts and character carefully because, in a real sense, we become the character we portray.

We were not born to be driven, controlled, shaped, and destined by a script that we did not write or choose. Rather, we can recognize our own destructive scripts and be freed from them. We can find contentment by letting go.

Chapter Five

OVERTHROW
THE TYRANNY
OF POSSESSIONS

IT IS HARD TO BELIEVE the skinny kid in that faded picture is really me. Imprinted on the serrated edge of the old black and white snapshot is a date, "November 1969." I am standing in front of my dorm during my freshman year in college.

Now, staring back into time, I find the length of my hair shocking. Shoulder-length, thick, and wild, it looks like a tangled lion's mane. My clothes startle and amuse me as well. Frayed bell-bottom jeans, a tie-dyed T-shirt, leather sandals, and a denim vest—believe me, I had to work hard to put that combination together. But it was the style and uniform of the day; a brisk slap in the face of American conventionality.

Over the years my generation has moved from being nonconformist, wealth-denying, back-to-the-earth hippies, to traditionalist, materialistic, conservative baby boomers. We've exchanged army surplus garb for Brooks Brothers suits. We've cut our hair and exposed our ears. We long ago traded our secondhand vans for expensive and trendy European cars. We've returned from the commune to the suburbs and are suddenly far more interested in "keeping up with the Joneses." In short, we have come full circle to embrace the values of our parents and the system we once ridiculed.

Holding the picture album in my hand, I realize I'm enjoying my nostalgia trip. An old James Taylor album is playing on the stereo, and as memories flood back on the wings of music, my eyes rest on the mahogany stereo speakers. A smile creases my lips and another image emerges.

Even if we claimed to be nonmaterialistic, we hippies loved our music. More than anything during my college years, I yearned for a fine stereo. But money was scarce, and I knew I would have to wait a while.

Beth and I were married soon after college graduation. Flat broke, we moved into an apartment devoid of furniture but full of love. With rough cinder blocks and bare boards we pieced our bookcases together, and we cooked in a cramped toaster oven. Furniture and appliances were beyond our means.

Several months after our wedding I made the mistake of walking by a stereo store that was having a bankruptcy liquidation sale. There in the window were two beautiful mahogany stereo speakers big enough to blow down the walls of any house—and they were reduced in price by 70 percent. I instantly knew I had to have those speakers.

Rushing home, I also knew I had to persuade Beth of the practicality of this impulse purchase. It would be an uphill battle. First of all, we had little money. Second, we had no turntable, amplifier, or tape deck. Finally, on our list of needs, a stereo was certainly not at the top. A mattress and box spring really had priority.

To my surprise I discovered that Beth had also lost her senses and was quite agreeable. With pride, we brought those sound blasters home and lugged them up the steps. As we placed them in the middle of our bare living room, we grinned at each other. They would make great end tables if only we had a couch. And they would produce wonderful music if only we had a stereo. But for now, well, we assured ourselves they were a great buy and a joy to look at.

More than a year later the mute speakers finally came to life with the purchase of a radio-amplifier. Slowly the apartment filled up with odds and ends until I graduated from seminary and we moved to another town and into a bigger house. Now—twenty-five years, four towns, four houses, and three children later—the two speakers stand all but forgotten, squeezed inconspicuously into corners of a room filled with furniture and toys.

Looking again at my college picture, I suddenly feel older, fatter, more middle-aged. Over the years Beth and I have accumulated a lot of stuff. And our appetites have only grown larger. What we have obtained has often only made us conscious of what we don't have. And we have never been happier than we were with an empty apartment filled with the silent music of contented hearts.

Memories aside, I have grudgingly come to see that I am as materialistic and possession-oriented as the next person. As a reactive young hippie, I denied it. As a fledgling Christian, I decried it. But now, at middle-age, I know it is true. I am driven to possess. And I believe most of us are.

It is widely recognized that our American culture surpasses all former ones in the accumulation of wealth, ease of lifestyle, and comfort of living. No other people have ever possessed so much. Yet, rather than be content and satisfied, we seem to be compulsively driven to possess more and more. And, tragically, our out-of-control need to acquire is robbing us of the pleasure of enjoying what we have and is causing us to destroy our lives.

Why do we have such a seemingly insatiable desire to possess? Why are we never satisfied? Let's consider these questions from both a biblical and a psychological perspective.

A Biblical Perspective

The Old Testament

We don't have to travel very far into the Bible before we come up against an inherent and unhealthy drive within men and women to possess what they do not have. In the opening chapters of the book of Genesis, we meet Adam and Eve living in a lush primeval garden in which every one of their basic needs is met. Not only are they physically cared for; they are free from the threat of war, disease, pestilence, and death. Life is full and complete, and they can even talk face to face with God.

But something is driving Adam and Eve crazy. God has told them that there is one thing in the garden they cannot have. Even though they can enjoy the fruit of many trees in the vast garden, there is one specific tree that God has said is off-limits. That tree is right in the middle of the garden and is called the Tree of the Knowledge of Good and Evil (Gen. 2:16–17).

It's an old and familiar story. The forbidden tree quickly moved from the center of the garden to the center of Adam's and Eve's thoughts. They became obsessively driven to possess what they didn't have. And that compulsion led to their downfall when they ate the forbidden fruit. In their quest to possess what they didn't have and weren't supposed to have, they destroyed what they did have and were forced out of the garden.

In this God-inspired story, we have a colorful picture of one of the basic characteristics of human nature. We tend to be destructively obsessed to obtain what we don't have. Mark Twain reflected on this in *The Tragedy of Pudd'nhead Wilson:* "Adam was but human—this explains it all. He did not want the apple for the apple's sake, he wanted it only because it was forbidden."[1]

Twain is right. And Genesis is right. And if the book of Genesis teaches us anything, it teaches us that an unabated and unbalanced drive to possess will separate us from enjoying what we do have and will cripple our lives.

The New Testament

As Jesus Christ strides across the pages of the New Testament, he is often a marvelous enigma and a stunning paradox. This is certainly true in his view of possessions and the material enjoyment of this world.

Jesus was certainly not what many devout religious figures of the first century envisioned when it came to piety and spiritual asceticism.

In complete contrast to his austere cousin John the Baptist, Jesus did not go around in camel's hair rags and eating a diet of locust and wild honey (Matt. 3:4). Rather, in the only place where Jesus' attire is described, he is wearing a seamless tunic—expensive clothing in his day (John 19:23-24).

Jesus' lifestyle and diet were not characteristic of the religious conservatives of those times either. Jesus seemed to love parties and wedding banquets. He graciously accepted, on occasion, certain extravagances from his followers (John 12:1-8). And the Pharisees publicly accused him of being "a glutton and a drunkard" (Matt. 12:19). Jesus was clearly a man who enjoyed life and ate and drank deeply of its rich substance.

Jesus was also glaringly not like certain of the religious sects of first-century Judaism that denied and rejected all personal possessions. Undoubtedly he was well aware of a large group of ascetic Jews called the Essenes, who lived in religious communes in the desert. They renounced all private possessions and refused to let their members own any personal property. Jesus could have followed their example. Yet, he obviously did not.

In contrast, when Jesus told his fishermen disciples to leave everything and follow him, he didn't insist they first sell their boats and homes. He just said, "Follow me." Many times over the years they returned to their boats, nets, homes, and families. They apparently retained their personal possessions. But they were learning to put Jesus Christ and his commandments first in their lives above everything else.

Rabbi Harold Kushner quotes from the rich wisdom of the ancient Jewish Talmud: "In the world to come, each of us will be called to account for all the good things God put on earth which we refused to enjoy."[2] I think Jesus would agree. Instead of being a radical like John the Baptist or an ascetic Essene, we are to enjoy fully "all the good things God put on the earth."

Yet, over against this, Jesus also sounded a loud note of responsibility and balance in the acquisition and enjoyment of possessions. He clearly states it is "easier for a camel to go through the eye of a needle than for a rich man to enter the Kingdom of God" (Mark 10:25). In the Sermon on the Mount, Jesus proclaims, "Do not lay up for your-selves treasures upon earth, where moth and rust destroy, and where thieves break in and steal; but lay up for yourselves treasures in heaven, where neither moth or rust destroys, and where thieves do not break in or steal; for where your treasure is, there will your heart be also" (Matt. 6:19-20).

Another time Jesus told a parable about a wealthy farmer who kept getting richer and richer. The larger his harvest grew, the more barns he built. Simply content to possess more and more, he devel-oped a philosophy of life in which he said, "Soul, you have many goods laid up for many years to come; take your ease, eat, drink and be merry." Yet God responded to this by saying, "You fool! This very night your soul is required of you; and now who will own what you have prepared?" And Jesus concludes the parable by reiterating his common theme, "So is the man who lays up treasures for himself, and is not rich toward God" (Luke 12:16-20).

How do we put these two contrasting sides of Jesus together? Are they compatible? I believe so.

Following the teachings in the Genesis story, Jesus believed that God created the world for men and women to enjoy fully. All that he created is inherently good. But once again, Jesus also affirmed that we recommit the sin of Adam and Eve when we become obsessed with possessing more and more and more, when we become slaves to "things."

Does this mean that it is wrong to accumulate wealth? No, I do not believe that Jesus would categorically denounce wealth. But he would ask some hard questions about how our abundance was used and where our heart is.

No, Jesus was not an ascetic. He enjoyed life fully and did not ask his followers to give up their personal possessions. But he did warn them that an insatiable desire to possess could be their downfall and that they would have to wrestle to become free from this inherent human trait.

A PSYCHOLOGICAL PERSPECTIVE

A Hierarchy of Needs

Psychologist Abraham Maslow has much to say about the drive to possess. In his seminal work, *Motivation and Personality,* Maslow establishes a concept he calls "a hierarchy of needs."[3] Within this framework of thought he proposes that men and women encounter accelerating and spiraling levels of human needs and possession requirements as they progress through life. Many of these needs are not physical or materialistic in nature.

At the first and most basic level in Maslow's scheme are physiological needs. These include such basics as food, water, oxygen, and shelter. After all, a person who is starving to death doesn't care whether he drives a used Ford or a new Mercedes Benz or even whether he drives at all. All that he is concerned with is possessing food to give him life for the present day. This is our primal need level.

Once our physiological needs are met, we move to a second level called safety needs. When we have been able to beat the odds and subsist on a survival level, we then want to establish a sense of order, defense, and dependability to assure ourselves of continuing safety. So we band together and create laws to ensure safety and predictability in the midst of a chaotic and unsafe world.

Once law and order are established we move to a third level of need, which Maslow calls "belongingness and love." As the hot adrenaline from danger and fear begins to recede from our veins, our natural human need for affection, appreciation, sexuality, familial warmth, and social acceptance floats to the surface of our awareness. We work hard to possess a feeling that we belong and that our relationships with others are secure.

Without sufficient satisfaction of love needs, we cannot develop further. Babies who do not receive loving care become fixated in their physical and mental development, even if their physiological and safety needs are met. These same relational needs continue through adulthood as well.

When our interpersonal needs have been adequately fulfilled and we feel basically loved, we are then able to move into a fourth level of need procurement, which Maslow calls esteem. The focus is increasingly on perceived self-identity. We have a growing need to possess self-esteem and self-respect, as well as to receive the esteem and respect of others. We usually gain esteem through achievements, possessions, and competence. We long to acquire prestige, recognition, acceptance, status, fame, and simple appreciation. The admiration and acceptance of others is important to us as we are learning to accept and affirm ourselves.

The final level of need fulfillment is what Maslow somewhat vaguely terms self-actualization. The basic emphasis here is that we are moving beyond our need to receive esteem from others and are instead more intent on actualizing or fulfilling our own perception of our needs and talents. We are more self-directed, and we now want to become all that we perceive we are capable of becoming, making full use of our talents, capacities, and potentials. In order to achieve this we must be able to recognize and engage our abilities and simultaneously satisfy our four lower-order needs. Dr. Maslow contends that the creative urge of self-actualization is a strong and unique striving of men and women.

Based on Maslow's hierarchy of need, it can be seen that our need to possess is never fulfilled. As soon as we struggle up the slopes of one stage of need fulfillment, we realize that we stand at the foot of another mountain of need to climb. Life is one long process of seeking to possess the fulfillment of our needs. Maslow gives us an interesting and intriguing framework to understand why we have this inherent and continuous drive to possess.

You Are What You Own

As we travel through Maslow's five levels of need requirements, we yearn to possess many material things. For instance, our forefathers concentrated on the primary level of physiological needs. I know that my great-great-great-grandfather must have longed for basic security as he cut paths through virgin forests across the new frontier of Kentucky. The material belongings he dreamed of having were such things as a rough log cabin stocked with game and produce. His prized possession might have been a rifle or a hand-tooled saddle.

Yet decades later, when streams have been forded, mountains crossed, the elements subdued, and cities built, we have gone beyond log cabins, rifles, and spinning wheels. Even a well-stocked pantry has receded in importance with the advent of supermarkets and frozen foods. For the most part we Americans take physiological needs and safety for granted. Our attention is focused primarily on esteem needs and self-fulfillment.

Social critics have called my generation the "Me Generation." Our popular magazine titles have symbolically evolved from *Life* to *People* to *Us* to *Self.* As a culture we are into esteem and self-fulfillment. Former President Ronald Reagan labeled our time "The Age of the Individual." We have become more self-centered.

As people struggle to climb the American mountain of esteem in a nation of plenty, it is easy to buy into the philosophy that "we are what we own." As we long to obtain the esteem and self-respect of others, we find it easy to believe that if we own the right thing, acquire certain symbolic possessions, then we—the people behind the possessions—will be well thought of and respected as well.

This is especially true for people who have struggled and crawled and limped up the perilous mountain or need level that, as noted, Maslow terms "belongingness and love." Most of us barely crested the summit, if we made it at all, before being thrown into another grueling uphill trek for esteem. Put another way, most of us never possessed adequate love or a sense of belonging. We never received enough "blessing" from parents or family and friends. And now, as we relentlessly attempt to satisfy our drive for esteem, we find it hard to believe we can be respected for simply being who we are. So we clothe and mask our naked insecurity with possessions, with a house in the right neighborhood, with the right car, and with the right labels on our clothes.

On my last birthday my wife gave me two beautiful sport shirts. Because I tend to be a little picky, Beth always says, "Now, you feel free to take them back and get what you really want," and I always grin and assure her they are perfect.

One of the shirts was similar to two others I already owned. So I took my birthday shirts back to the store on my next trip to the mall. The shirts were the store brand and the salesman was proud of them. He carefully showed me how thick the material was and how it was double-stitched like the shirts "that cost twice as much." Then, when his store-label sales pitch was finished, he pointed at the more costly shirts in a colorful display nearby, and I walked over to look at them.

He was right. They were identical. The quality was the same. And then I noticed it. My two shirts didn't have a designer crest on the front. That was the difference.

Several minutes later I walked sheepishly out of the store, bag in hand. I had bought the designer shirt. I traded two shirts for one.

Why did I do it? Well, to quote myself as I stood with a red face and told Beth what I'd done, "I just decided to throw care to the wind and buy what I truly wanted." And that was the truth. But why did I want the more expensive shirt? You guessed it. The lure of trend, the desire for image, an ingrained belief that "you are what you own."

As we have looked at the testimony of the Bible as well as some of the insights of modern psychology, we have seen one common theme emerge: We have a deep and compelling need to possess what we do not have; to garner esteem by what we do not own. We are slaves to an insatiable appetite to possess.

DANGERS WITHIN THE DRIVE TO POSSESS

As we are driven to possess, we must see (as did Adam and Eve) that there are some very real dangers inherent in our quest. Although a desire to possess is not necessarily evil, when possessions begin to take control of our life we face very real perils. What are some of these dangers?

Illusion

Not long ago I read a statement that stopped me cold: "My problem is not that you cannot have what you think you want; the problem is that when you get what you think you want, it won't satisfy." As I reflected on this statement, I realized that one of the major problems in our society is not acquisition but illusion.

Many of us dream of things we have yearned to possess for a long time. And as we picture those things we want so desperately, we are driven to work and slave and save. We budget and juggle our finances until at last we buy what we want. It is then that we slowly discover the grand illusion. What we have finally possessed will not satisfy.

Nothing is more piercing to me as a parent than to see the unavoidable dawning of a painful truth strike home in the life of my children. I remember when my oldest son was five years old and, much to my chagrin, became mesmerized by the He-Man craze. He longed to collect every one of these grotesquely muscular, bigger-than-life characters. He knew them all by name. As Christmas drew near he became aware that He-Man's headquarters, Castle Grayskull, was being produced by a toy company. When Drew saw Castle Grayskull advertised on television his imagination went wild. He had to have this glorious castle, and he placed it at the top of his Christmas list.

I tried subtly to change Drew's mind. This mound of plastic was much too expensive. It would be difficult to assemble, and it would be constantly underfoot. But how do you dissuade a wide-eyed five-year-old? At best I could simply say, "Well, Santa will have to decide."

Two nights before Christmas I found myself in a huge toy warehouse battling savagely for one of the few remaining Castle Grayskulls in town. The advertising paid off. There had been a mad grab for this popular item, and I was in the midst of the fray. I was suddenly willing to pay twice the price to secure it.

True to my expectations, it nearly took a structural engineer to put the thing together. But when it was all over with and under the Christmas tree, I couldn't wait to see Drew's bright eyes.

Sure enough, his eyes were wide and radiant. But they didn't stay that way long. For a week Castle Grayskull was in great demand. But then, strangely, Drew began to return to his old wooden blocks and build his own versions of "He-Man's house." Castle Grayskull sat silently and forgotten in the corner. A few years ago, it disappeared, sold in the midst of a garage sale.

Why? Well, I sort of suspect that nothing could have fulfilled Drew's childlike expectations. Molded plastic just could not house the likes of He-Man in the unbounded imagination of this little child. The illusion was richer than the possession.

How many times do we adults buy into the same folly? We purchase a lakefront house to improve our family life. We slave away and pay for an advanced academic degree to give us esteem and position. We buy the dress, or the piece of furniture, or the Mercedes, and for a week, a month, or a year, we are excited. And then we are empty. Why is it that more often than not when we get what we want, it doesn't satisfy?

Let's face it—few possessions can match the level of our expectations. And no material possession can take the place of love and respect and give us esteem. The quicker we learn this truth through the hard knocks of experience, the better we will be able to moderate our drive to possess.

Appreciation

In the opening pages of his classic novel, *The Portrait of a Lady,* Henry James depicts an aging American sitting on a large manor lawn in England. Mr. Touchett had come to England as a young man and made a sensational fortune. Now retired and convalescing, he sits drinking tea in the warmth of the sun.

A young friend, Lord Warburton, stands beside him. Looking at the elderly man, Warburton remarks, "You look wonderfully comfortable."

Mr. Touchett replies, "Well, I suppose I am, in most respects. The fact is I've been comfortable so many years that I suppose I've got so used to it I don't know it."

"Yes, that's the bore of comfort," said Lord Warburton. "We only know when we're uncomfortable."[4]

When I first read these lines I felt a sneering grin creep across my face. A conversation like that could only occur between wealthy gentry who were so out of touch with reality as to be absurd. But as I reflected further on this conversation written more than a century ago, I realized that it applies just as well to the average American of today. Most of us have been so blessed by material things that we do experience "the bore of comfort."

There is danger hidden within our incessant drive to possess: In our accumulation of so many things, we lose our appreciation for what we have. We develop a sense of acquisition numbness, a boredom that deadens our ability to appreciate what we have received.

Recently I revisited the old historic district of Charleston, where my family had lived for seven years when the children were small, to take a midnight stroll. Walking amid the beautiful eighteenth-century houses, I imagined what it would have been like to live two hundred years ago.

It was a hot and humid evening, and as I walked I listened to the quiet hum of air conditioners. How uncomfortable it must have been before air conditioning to lie listless in a feather bed waiting for a dank, tepid sea breeze to move stagnant air. And without screens at the windows, the mosquitoes would have been unbearable.

When I stepped off the curb to cross a street, I thought about the muddy streets of two hundred years ago. I smelled stale excrement from only one errant tour carriage horse and wondered what the daily traffic flow of a thousand horses and wagons would smell like. Then when I thought about several thousand backyard privies, I turned my mind to more pleasant things.

Walking on, I strained to read a dimly lit street sign. Without my modern contact lenses, I would be legally blind. Without good dental care, I am confident that all but two or three of my teeth would have long been gone. I thought of the childhood diseases I had survived—measles, mumps, chicken pox, flu, hepatitis, and dysentery. Any one could have easily killed me if I had been born two hundred years ago. Again, I thought of something more pleasant.

When I arrived back at our bed-and-breakfast inn and saw my car parked under the streetlight, I knew that my pastor predecessors would have been awestruck by that mechanical marvel. How in the world did they do their work without a car or telephone or secretary?

By the time I stepped into the door of our house I knew what Mr. Touchett meant when he said, "I've been comfortable so many years that I suppose I've got so used to it I don't know it."

There is a real danger lurking within our passionate drive to possess. We can be so busy pursuing what we do not have that we rob ourselves of the enjoyment and appreciation of what is ours. And that is a tragic shame.

Destruction

As a little boy I was transfixed by the beauty of bright new spring flowers. Getting down on my knees, I looked closely at their petals and smelled their fragrance. I instinctively wanted to possess that beauty, to grasp the flowers in my hand and take them with me. So I picked them, put them in a water-filled jelly jar, and proudly gave them to my mother.

It was then that I learned one of life's major lessons. Within hours the flowers wilted and died. In my attempt to possess living beauty for myself, I discovered I had killed the very life-source of that beauty.

How many times has the appreciation of a person—be it a friend, an infatuation, a sweetheart, or even a spouse—been ruined and its life-source uprooted by our desire to possess and to control? Suddenly, beautiful human beings who voluntarily coexist with us and freely share their beauty become "my" best friend, "my" girlfriend, "my" child, or even "my" wife or husband. The emphasis is not so much on the relationship—even a relationship based on clearly perceived mutual commitment such as marriage—but rather on the possessive pronoun "my."

I remember a night long ago when fireflies made their annual debut across a summer sky. Our two little boys were mesmerized.

Grabbing canning jars from the pantry, Drew and Luke ran outside to capture the fireflies and make firefly lanterns. Sitting on the porch, we cut holes in the jar lids so the little beetles could breathe. And then for an hour we sat back and watched the phosphorescent wonder of these amazing insects.

Finally it was time for bed. Drew and Luke wanted to take their firefly lanterns to bed with them. It was then, however, that I had to explain that we needed to take the lids off of the jars and let the fireflies go. If we didn't, the fireflies would die and their lights would go out forever.

Being little boys, they struggled to understand this. In their own "me-oriented" world, they could not understand that some things can only be possessed when they are given their freedom. Slowly, however, they acquiesced and we walked outside. With a sense of joy, we all celebrated as the fireflies slowly left the jar and were free to move out into the darkness with their lights sparkling in the night.

There are some things in life that cannot be possessed. And these things are living, breathing, creations of God. We do well to remember that our quest to possess the living always ends in the destruction of life and beauty.

Enslavement

Just as fireflies can be placed in a jar, so can we also be imprisoned and enslaved by our possessions. There is a little ditty I learned somewhere that goes, "Possessions weigh me down in life; I never feel quite free. I wonder if I own my things, or if my things own me."

I have thought about this recently. I remember that when I was a six-year-old my father and my mother felt that God was leading them to be missionaries in Southeast Asia. By the age of thirty-eight, my parents had collected many things. To move to a foreign land was a major decision. It meant selling most of what we owned.

I remember the day we had the big household sale. People started arriving early in the morning, and by the end of the day most of our household possessions had been sold. Today I wonder if I would have my parents' courage and commitment. I wonder—do I own my things or do my things own me?

In an affluent society such as we enjoy, where we tend to define ourselves by what we own, we have too often become a people enslaved by security and possessions. We build large houses that become prisons as we strain to pay high mortgage payments. Then we go on to fill those houses with equally beautiful furnishings. And, of course, our yards must make a statement about who we are. So, during every free minute, we are mowing the lawn, pruning shrubs, fertilizing the grass, painting the fence, repairing the house—doing all the things that "must be done." In this frantic process children are neglected, our golf clubs collect dust, and the thought of spending an afternoon quietly reading or fishing is inconceivable. We have unwittingly become slaves to our possessions.

When my parents were appointed as missionaries, the executive secretary of the Southern Baptist Foreign Mission Board was the late Dr. Baker James Cauthen. Through the years I've heard this vibrant man speak many times. There is one story he told that I will never forget.

Dr. and Mrs. Cauthen went to China as missionaries during their early thirties. Soon after they arrived their work was interrupted by the outbreak of World War II. They had to leave north China immediately, abandoning everything they owned except for what they could carry in their hands. They knew they would never see their possessions again.

In telling this story many years later, Dr. Cauthen spoke of how he had expected to have a deep, wrenching feeling of panic, anger, grief, and sorrow. Instead he was overcome with a sense of freedom. It was as if a weight had been lifted from his shoulders. For the first time in his life he felt unencumbered by possessions, and a strange sense of peace filled his heart. He then concluded, "Carry your possessions in your hands, but not in your hearts."

Now I am certainly not suggesting that we should burn our possessions, sell our houses, or quit tending our yards. But it is important to see that our possessions can hold us hostage and keep us from being all that we are meant to be.

Blindness

Several years ago I was standing on a dock looking out across the Atlantic Ocean and talking to an old fisherman. As we conversed, some large pelicans flew overhead in perfect formation. Commenting on these amazing birds, I said, "I wonder what the age span of a pelican is?" The fisherman gave a curious reply, "It depends on how good their eyes are."

When I asked the old man what he meant, he told me an interesting story. It seems that pelicans do not have eyelids. Therefore, when diving to catch fish, they cannot cover and shield their eyeballs from the harsh impact of the water. Consequently over a period of years, their eyes are slowly traumatized until they grow blind. When the big lumbering birds can no longer see their source of food, they starve to death.

In recent days I have thought of this story as I have reflected on some of the dangers inherent in our human drive to possess. Like the pelicans, all of us go through life trying desperately to fill our own hunger and emptiness. Like the pelicans, we dive and dive and dive after our own perception of what possessions will satisfy us. However, in our self-centered quests we are not aware that we are slowly becoming blind to the realities of the world around us. We are so intent on our driving need to possess that we unwittingly become blind to the larger needs of our world and, as a result, we starve to death spiritually.

This analogy is not perfect, but the truth shines through. One of the real dangers of constantly seeking our own possessions is that we grow increasingly unaware of human need around us and in our world. I am convinced that if every Christian gave only a small percentage of his or her income annually to minister to worldwide hunger, starvation in our world would be greatly reduced, if not eradicated, within our lifetime. Yet we are so busy diving for our own fish that we create within ourselves a blinding spiritual insensitivity.

I believe this is the reason Jesus placed so much stress on sharing our possessions. As we have seen, Jesus did not tell his disciples to renounce their possessions. Rather, he taught them to share what they had with the poor and needy.

In an intriguing passage in the Sermon on the Mount, Jesus instructs his disciples with these words:

> "The lamp of the body is the eye; if therefore your eye is clear, your whole body will be full of light. But it your eye is bad, your whole body will be full of darkness. If therefore the light that is in you is darkness, how great is the darkness. No one can serve two masters; for either he will hate the one and love the other, or he will hold to one and despise the other. You cannot serve God and riches [mammon]." (Matt. 6:22-24)

How cogently did Jesus understand the tragic truth of "pelican-itis." When our eye goes bad, we cannot see the world around us. We begin to serve one master. We accumulate possessions and forget the needs of others. Slowly, we die spiritually.

The real danger of possessions is not the possessions themselves or our enjoyment of them. The danger is that we will not see the needs of others and share with them.

LIVING WITH THE DRIVE TO POSSESS

As we have seen, our inherent and obsessive drive to possess is revealed in the Bible and substantiated by modem psychology. Though possessions as such are not evil, they present us some very real dangers. Consequently we must ask ourselves, "How can we live in this world, enjoy fully its beautiful treasures, and not be disillusioned, enslaved, or blinded by our drive to possess?" Many times, we can only find contentment by letting go of a lifestyle that ensnares us.

Developing a Sense of Gratitude

Perhaps one of the best ways to combat an insatiable drive to possess is to develop within ourselves a conscious and deliberate sense of gratitude. It is a strange paradox that people who live in affluent societies are often the most lacking in appreciation. Because of this, the affluent person is also frequently empty and depressed. If there is any one thing that can bring feelings of happiness and well-being into our lives, it is the intentional cultivation of thanksgiving.

Observing this, Elisabeth Elliot writes, "It is always possible to be thankful for what is given rather than to complain about what is not given. One or the other becomes a habit of life."[5] She is right. We will either develop a natural tendency to be thankful or an empty heart that will relentlessly drive us to possess more and more. And we can choose which "habit" we will develop.

In order to help Christians develop a healthy perspective of thanksgiving, the early church fathers would teach them to order their prayers in a four-step sequence. First, they were taught to thank God for all that he had given them. Second, they were to confess their sins openly before their Father. Third, they were to pray for others who were in need. Then, only after completing these first three steps, were they free to take the fourth step: pray for their own needs.

The wisdom in following this form of prayer is that it directs us to put the world in the proper perspective. After we have completed the first three steps of this prayer form, we are suddenly brought to an awareness of how fortunate we really are. Only then are we in a proper frame of mind to ask God for what we need.

For some time now I have practiced this form of prayer every morning. I keep a journal in which I daily record my thanksgiving, my confession, my prayers of intercession for others, and, finally, my requests for myself. I can honestly say that this discipline has made a significant difference in my life. I've sensed that my feelings of gratitude have become stronger, and my drive to possess has waned in influence.

George Herbert was an English clergyman and poet who worked and wrote during the early seventeenth century. Though he lived to be only forty, he discovered the secret of happiness that came from an attitude of thanksgiving. With words still fresh he wrote to his God, "Thou who has given so much to me, give one thing more—a grateful heart. . . ."[6] This prayer can set us free from the tyranny of possession to discover the luxury and freedom of contentment and appreciation.

Discovering the Secret of Giving

I recently read a wonderful book entitled *The Education of Little Tree* by Forrest Carter.[7] It is the story of a young Native American boy named Little Tree. When Little Tree is left an orphan, he is sent to live with his Cherokee grandparents in the Smokey Mountains. Soon the wizened grandfather begins to teach Little Tree about the way of his people.

One day grandfather and grandson went hunting. The old man dug a hole in the ground and made a turkey trap. When they returned hours later, six turkeys were gobbling in the trap.

All six turkeys were removed from the trap and their legs securely bound. As they lay squawking and flapping on the ground, the grandfather told Little Tree that they only needed three turkeys. Then he went on to explain that they should choose the three smallest and least likely to survive and set the others free to reproduce and provide food for someone else. In this graphic way Little Tree learned that the way of his people is to be as concerned with giving to life as much as taking from life. He never forgot the lesson of that day. Nor have I.

In our affluent, Western, industrialized societies, we have too often forgotten the way of the Indians. And we have forgotten the way of Jesus Christ as well.

It is interesting that one verse in every six in the first three Gospels relates, either directly or indirectly, to money and possessions. Sixteen of our Lord's forty-four parables speak of the use or misuse of possessions. And always the message is the same: share with others.

Why is it so important to share with others? One reason is apparent. In sharing, we help others. But a second reason is not so apparent until it is experienced. In sharing we also help ourselves. Through sharing, our drive to possess is somehow diluted, and we are free to direct new energy toward helping others. It is in this process that we discover the spiritual paradox: in giving we receive.

Reflecting on the myth that it is financial independence that makes us free, Erich Fromm made this perceptive observation, "Not he who has much is free, but he who gives much."[8] Fromm knew

what Little Tree discovered and Jesus proclaimed. The greatest freedom in life is found when we are not driven to possess and hoard but
are released to give freely of what we have. Giving fills our emptiness;
simply receiving depletes our soul.

Discovering the Things That Are Free

We can further moderate our desire to possess by realizing that most
of the finest things in life are free.

Several years ago I was fortunate to visit the Prado in Madrid, the
art museum where the paintings of Francisco Goya are exhibited.
Quite unexpectedly I was moved to tears by the pathos and tragedy
of scenes Goya painted of the French invasion of Spain. Those scenes
are vivid in my memory today.

Obviously, I will never be able to afford a Goya painting, even if
it was for sale. But I don't need to, because the gift of his art is etched
in my mind and heart. It was a gift free of charge.

It is so true that the very best things in life are free. For me those
things are sunsets and salty ocean spray, the warmth of a fire, the
laughter of a child, the joy of infatuation, the embrace of a lover, and
the gentle knowledge of the presence of God. All of these things are
absolutely priceless. Any attempt to possess them and make them
mine would be destructive. Yet they can be received by all.

Sometimes when the money in my pocket burns and another
"I've got to have it" binge is at hand, I take a few moments to think
of all the good things in life that are free. Somehow, some way, these
thoughts return my vision to its proper perspective, and I am released
from the tyranny to possess.

· · · · · · · · · ·

Our discussion has made us aware that to be human is to be driven
to possess. We know, of course, that material possessions can enhance
and enrich our lives. But when the acquisition of possessions
becomes a driving and obsessive force in our lives, then we are in

danger of committing the sin of Adam and Eve. To do that is to allow our material possessions to separate us from the true meaning and value of a life that is free to experience the abundant richness of God. We can find true contentment only by slowly letting go of our need to possess.

Chapter Six

CONNECT WITH OTHERS

T O BE AFLOAT IN THE MIDDLE OF A VAST OCEAN, hundreds of miles from land, is an awesome experience. It is breathtaking to gaze at a 360-degree horizon and realize that only a thin planked hull is separating you from the watery deep.

In Herman Melville's day the whaling ships would often lower their sails and drift momentarily in the water to allow the crew to clamber overboard and take a bath. Describing such a moment, Melville writes:

> Now, in calm weather, to swim in the open ocean is as easy to the practiced swimmer as to ride in a spring-carriage ashore. But the awful lonesomeness is intolerable. The intense concentration of the self in the middle of such a heartless immensity, my God!, who can tell it? Mark, how when sailors in a dead calm bathe in the open sea—mark how closely they hug their ship and only coast along the side.[1]

To be adrift in a vast ocean, even within arm's length of safety, is an anxious experience. We all fear being abandoned.

In *Moby Dick* one of Captain Ahab's crew was a young cabin boy named Pip. Possessed of a very lively and effervescent personality, Pip was a favorite among the whalers. Even though theirs was a hard life, Pip seemed to never have a care in the world.

Because of his youth and inexperience, Pip was never called upon to man the small pursuit boats to chase and harpoon the whales. One day, however, one of the oarsmen grew ill and Pip was ordered to replace him. When a whale was sighted, Pip's pursuit boat was lowered into the water and soon engaged the whale. Quickly a harpoon was thrust deep into the mammal's flank, and the frantic animal began to rapidly tow the boat like a skier behind a ski boat.

In the midst of the frenzied activity, the inexperienced Pip got entangled in the harpoon line as it was being furiously reeled out by the fleeing whale. Like a rag doll in the hand of a giant, he was viciously thrown out of the boat. But because the boat was attached to the whale by the harpoon and rope, the crew couldn't abandon the chase to rescue Pip. In a few moments the small pursuit boat disappeared and Pip was left alone and terrified in the midst of the vast ocean.

Though Pip was later rescued, the trauma of his abandonment caused him to lose his sanity. Melville described the scene in a few cryptic words: "By the merest chance the ship itself rescued him; but from that hour the little Negro went about the deck an idiot; such, at least they said he was. The sea had jeeringly kept his finite body up, but drowned the infinite of his soul."[2] Truly, to be a human being is to feel to varying degrees the primal fear of aloneness, of separation from others. When this pain is intense, it does threaten to "drown the infinite of the soul."

Pip's harrowing experience is told in a chapter Melville appropriately titled "The Castaway." Dredging up the elemental truth of life, Melville knew that in reality all men and women are castaways. Huddled on a tiny, spinning clod of matter called Earth, we are seemingly lost and abandoned in the infinite immensity of space. We are truly cosmic castaways.

The Psalmist sensed this truth of human existence when he wrote, "When I consider Thy heavens, the work of Thy fingers, The moon and the stars, which Thou hast ordained; what is man, that Thou dost take thought of him?" (8:3-4). To be adrift in the middle of the ocean or to meditate on the immensity of space gives us the strange feeling that we are all castaways.

The realization of our profound separation comes to us much earlier than our adult musings upon the ocean and the sky. Our first experience of life is one of traumatic divorce—of being squeezed and pushed and pulled from the warm symbiosis of the womb and having our umbilical cord severed from the very life that has conceived and sustained us. Psychiatrists and psychologists agree that this moment of separation subconsciously affects each day that we live. Deep within our psyche there is a memory of when we were one with somebody else—united in heartbeat and blood flow and flesh. Throughout our lives we are driven to find that unity again.

Reflecting the literary insight of Melville and the Moby Dick story in a more scientific way, the renowned personality theorist Erich Fromm writes, "The experience of separateness arouses anxiety; it is, indeed, the source of all anxiety. . . . The deepest need of man, then, is the need to overcome his separateness, to leave the prism of his aloneness. The absolute failure to do this means insanity."[3]

There is little doubt that perhaps the greatest desire of people everywhere—the most prevalent cause of our relentless drivenness is to "leave the prison of our aloneness" and experience unity again. In the midst of our ocean, we want to climb aboard ship again. And in the midst of life, we never cease hungering for that oneness we experienced in our mother's womb.

Although the quest for unity is universal and healthy, this compelling drive can take us down some dangerous dead-end streets and compel us to follow some futile pursuits. Indeed many of our frantic attempts to find unity in our world often only accentuates our loneliness. Thirsting in the midst of the vast ocean, we foolishly drink salt water to relieve our craving. To find contentment, we need to assess our drive toward relationships and fully understand the promises as well as the pitfalls of the anxious quests we pursue. Let's move in now for a close look at five routes we can take in our quest toward unity.

QUESTS TOWARD UNITY

Friendship and Marriage

Francis Bacon once said that "the worst solitude is to be destitute of sincere friendship."[4] He is absolutely right. One of the healthiest approaches toward alleviating the gnawing sense of loneliness within us is to develop friendships. Truly, friendships form some of the very richest experiences of life. Indeed, the ability to initiate and sustain meaningful friendships is one of the key indicators of emotional and psychological health.

And yet most of us have also experienced the pain of disappointment and the hurt resulting from friendships turned sour. Reflecting on such pain, the sometimes caustic philosopher Jean-Paul Sartre brashly declared, "Hell is other people!"[5] Perhaps this is an overstatement. But the person who has never experienced the hellish pain of a shipwrecked friendship has not lived long enough or deep enough.

Earlier I referred to a book entitled *Necessary Losses,* by Judith Viorst. In this work, Viorst shows that a very basic need in making it through the adult years is to come to terms with and find acceptance of certain inevitable losses and griefs. One of these "necessary losses" is an overly idealized view of friendship. Commenting on this, Viorst states:

> For we once believed that our friends were our friends only when our love and trust were absolute, when we shared identical tastes and passions and goals, when we felt that we could bare the darkest secrets of our souls with utter impunity, when we willingly would run—no questions asked—to help each other in times of trouble. We once believed that our friends were our friends only when they fit that mythic model. But growing up means giving up that view. For even if we are lucky enough to have one or two or three beloved "best friends," friendships, we learn, are at best an imperfect connection.[6]

Due to our aching loneliness, we are driven down a healthy path toward friendship. But sooner or later we must all come to realize that as good and as rich as friendships can be at times, they are "imperfect connections."

Perhaps another term that should be linked to Viorst's concept of "imperfect connections" is the term *over-expectation*. In my experience, unrealistic demands often cause our relationships with other people to founder and grow unhealthy.

Many of us latch on to new friendships like a drowning person clutching a floating timber. We have been slaves to loneliness for so long that when an opportunity for friendship drifts our way, we cling to it as if our life depends on it. This same reaction is also frequently seen in a marriage relationship. We are so sure that this friend—and even this marriage partner—is going to be the missing piece to our life-puzzle, the once-and-for-all answer to our feelings of aloneness and alienation. We're convinced that now the severed umbilical cord of infancy will be sutured and we'll be whole again.

But this is an over-expectation for either friendship or marriage. No human relationship can possibly fill all of the loneliness within our lives. And if we expect it to—indeed demand that it does—we will destroy what comfort friendship or marriage can realistically bring.

Many times in conversation with young married couples I've heard the question, "What is wrong with our marriage?" As a rule, the couple does need to confront some real difficulties and make certain adjustments. But almost inevitably one of the biggest problems is one of over-expectation. After the honeymoon is over they are shocked—and angrily disappointed—that feelings of loneliness are still present, that complete oneness has not been achieved, and that the pain of separation still exists even after vows and rings have been exchanged.

Though expectations in friendship are not as high as in marriage relationships, we still silently shout in the midst of an intimate dinner party, "Why am I so lonely?" In our inner restlessness and desperation we long for that friendship to come along that will adequately fill our emptiness and satisfy our emotional hunger.

Several years ago I found myself struggling with this feeling. Beth and I had returned from a lovely evening spent with some of our very closest friends. Feeling warmed and filled by the experience, we came home to a quiet house and a sleeping baby-sitter. After taking the baby-sitter home, I drove to our house aware of an overwhelming sense of loneliness. I felt as if I wanted to cry. It seemed as if the intimacy of the evening—the closeness of friendship—had only awakened a deeper level of hunger for relationships.

Later that night as Beth and I lay in bed, I couldn't shed my stark feelings of loneliness. Caressing the sleeping warmth of a woman I deeply loved, and listening to the even breathing of our children nearby, I felt silly feeling alone and isolated. And yet the feeling persisted. Finally I slipped out of bed and went to my desk. Taking pencil and paper, I began to write a prayer. Slowly these words emerged:

> Dear God,
>
> I have tried to write this prayer at least a dozen times. Weeks have gone by between attempts. Yet, with each fresh start I have put my pencil down to await a clearer mind or a more inspired moment. And still, words fail me.
>
> How can I speak of the loneliness within me, O Lord? I, who have been blessed with a loving wife, affectionate children, quality friendships, and a caring Heavenly Father—how can I speak of loneliness? And yet, it is there, O Lord. A feeling of separation that stifles my tongue and spirit.
>
> It seems that loneliness is the thorn of all flesh. The curse of Eden. Somehow I always thought it would get better. And over the years, I guess, it has. But the pain still nags and throbs beneath the surface of my smile.
>
> Do you remember when I was a little boy, O Father, and Steve would come over to spend the night? In the darkness, we would giggle and tell silly jokes. Fighting sleep together, we experienced a closeness of friendship I have never known in manhood. I long for those days of "best friends."

And then there were team sports and clubs. Girls and dating. And finally, the pinnacle, marriage. And yet, even in marriage, the closer Beth and I have become—the more we share ourselves in our children, our dreams, our fears, and our convictions—the more I realize there is a distance between two people that cannot be wholly breached by love, or sexual union, or anything upon this earth. To touch one you really love with your eyes or your thoughts or a gentle kiss is to know a beckoning distance.

O Lord, give me the ability to live amidst loneliness with a thankful heart for all of the beautiful relationships that I have shared but not possessed. Give me the wisdom to know that loneliness is but the suction of the heart that draws us toward God. I pray this in the name of Him who said, "The foxes have holes, and the birds of the air have nests, but the Son of Man has nowhere to lay His head."

AMEN.[7]

In that midnight moment I came to realize that friendships and marriage cannot totally remove my loneliness. And to expect them to—to demand that they do—is to destroy the rich solace that they can bring. To accept this reality is to grieve. But not to accept it is to be a driven person whose intensity and over-expectation destroys the relationships we value most. Contentment is found when we let go of unrealistic expectations of relationships.

Sexuality

Another healthy and normal quest to bridge our loneliness is through sexuality. The sexual drive, passion, and resulting union between [people] is God-given. The sexual act was created for far more than biological procreation. Sex is also for the purpose of pleasure, excitement, and intimacy. And God said, "It is good."

There are few times in our life when we feel alienation more keenly than in adolescence. Yet, as young teenagers, something new and wonderful also begins to change within us. Our hormones alter their delicate balance. The sap of vitality begins to rise within us. Bothersome members of the opposite sex suddenly become the most lovely creatures in the world.

Perhaps there is nothing else in life quite as rich as our first mutual infatuation. Knuckles touch, clammy hands are nervously held, there is the first brush of lips roughly resembling a kiss, and suddenly the most marvelous realization in the world explodes—"I love her and she loves me!" For the first time, walls that separate are torn down. There is a delicious feeling of wanting to draw closer and closer. We embrace each other tighter and tighter, hoping to merge into one.

Suddenly the thoughts of sexual intercourse are not the result of asking, "Momma, where do babies come from?" Rather, the desire for sexual union is as natural as breathing. Left to our own devices we would experience sexual intercourse in early adolescence.

But other forces usually restrain us from early sexual union. There are tribal rites and social taboos. There is family jurisdiction and propriety. But above all, there is religious teaching. And for many people—Christians, Jews, and Muslims—sexual intercourse is not to be experienced outside of the marriage commitment.

Like a child on December twenty-sixth longing for the next Christmas, an intolerable distance away, the sixteen-year-old wonders how it will be to hold another and to become one. The reputation of orgasm begins to build to mythic height. Hollywood, Madison Avenue advertising, television, clothing styles, the clandestine actions and reports of our sexually active friends, all tell us that sexual intercourse—or whatever less formal word is in vogue—is so very wonderful.

And it is! We get married and discover that it is. Orgasm is indeed the closest experience we have ever known of merging two souls into one. But it happens so fast and is over so quickly.

Attempting to improve on a good thing, we read all available books on sex. We try everything that is suggested, but deep within we begin to feel a subtle grief that we do not know how to express.

Why grief? Is uninhibited sexual experience not wonderful? In all honesty, it certainly is. "But is that all?" the little child asks, surrounded by toys and up to his chin in wrapping paper on Christmas Day. We realize that in our healthy drivenness toward a very good thing, we have once again set ourselves up for disappointment.

As with friendship, the sexual relationship is laden with impossible over-expectations. True, it is a wonderful experience—a wonderful taste or appetizer of the relational union that is to be beyond the horizon of this life. But the American sexual myth has promised a complete meal that is totally filling. And when we still hunger, we grieve.

Rather than readjusting expectation, many people continue to be recklessly driven. Total sexual fulfillment must be found in another partner or with many partners. And so on the drivenness goes. Unable to enjoy the wonderful experience that sex truly is, the driven person focuses on the grief of what sex is not. He or she is constantly in search of a better friend, a better mate, a better experience. One day, though, this sexually-driven person wakes up in the midst of broken lives and dreams to belatedly accept the fact that sex is great but has its limitations.

Yes, the quest for sexual union is good and healthy. But soon we must discover that sex is not the panacea we thought it would be. Once we have let go of our unreasonable expectations, we are free to experience the wonder and the passion of a healthy sexual life.

Truth

As we are driven by our loneliness toward unity through friendship and sexuality, we are also directed toward a quest for truth. Along with the ancient Greek philosophers, we sense that there is a level of ultimate truth that is unchanging. By grasping hold of this truth with our reason, we believe we can hold on to something that is timeless and permanent.

When Jesus was brought before Pontius Pilate, this Roman sensed that Jesus was someone special. He therefore asked him a classic question: "What is truth?" (John 18:38). Pilate wanted Jesus to give him a philosophic argument that would point to ultimate truth. Instead Jesus stood in silence. He refused to give the impression that truth could be grasped totally by reason. Rather than speaking the truth, Jesus insisted that he embodied the truth.

In recent centuries the search for philosophic truth has broadened to include the sphere of science. The scientist believes that there are certain unalterable natural laws and principles. And even if the human race ceased to exist, natural law would continue indefinitely. It is thought that even though history changes, natural law remains constant.

Throughout history men and women have attempted to quiet the anxiety of their impermanence—the awareness that they are finite and must die—by mentally grasping hold of eternal truths. By penetrating the ultimate, we hope vicariously to be united to the essence of the infinite.

But the greatest problem we face in our search for truth is that the more we penetrate the ultimate, the more we realize how little we know. The wisest people are aware that they understand so very little, that we are surrounded by mystery. And so our quest toward union through the knowledge of ultimate truth comes full circle to the confession of our ignorance. We still face the world as human beings who know they are finite, but yearn to be connected to the infinite. Union with truth eludes us all.

Relationship with God

In our search for ultimate truth, many of us turn to a belief in God. Indeed, we move beyond a sterile philosophic belief in God to develop what might be called a "personal relationship" with God. We begin to talk about God using personal terms such as *father* or *friend* or *shepherd*. These are terms that point to the fact that God can be a close relational presence in our lives.

However, as with all friendships, we are frustrated at times by a sense of distance in our relationships. Our relationship with God is no different. God is often experienced as much by distance as by presence. God is felt as much by the pain of his absence as the intimacy of his closeness.

Many of us who have been spiritually driven toward God become frustrated when our relationship with God is not as close as we desire it to be. We feel guilty about this and make commitments to deepen our prayer life and spend more time in meditation and reflection. Frequently we grow guilty, thinking that something is wrong with us; that we are spiritually insensitive. Ultimately, we can grow frustrated and sometimes be prone to decide that our lack of intimacy with God must mean that God does not exist.

However, the greatest saints have often said that God is like a great mountain. From a distance, the mountain seems accessible. However, the closer we get to the mountain, the higher it seems, the more impossible it appears to scale, the more removed is its summit. Likewise, the closer we draw to God, the greater is God's awesome mystery, the more unfathomable his ways, the more we are aware that we are at a distance from God.

Thus we enter the spiritual paradox that the more we penetrate God's mystery, the greater the mystery becomes. The closer we draw unto God, the more that we realize his Holy distance. We must accept the fact that though God is our intimate Father who loves us, He is also a Great God that our minds and souls cannot fully comprehend.

Legacy and Immortality

Having watched friends and loved ones die and pass into the unknown, men and women throughout the centuries have reached out for some vestiges of immortality upon the earth. The fear of separation by death can be partially quelled if we feel like we are leaving a segment of ourselves behind when it is our turn to die.

One of the classic ways by which men and women have sought immortality is through their children. There is a feeling that even though we are separated by death, we live on through our children.

I remember vividly having a very fulfilling sense of relief when my first son was born. I had a definite awareness that if I were to die, I would not simply disappear without any trace. My son—the flesh of my flesh—would continue on.

Another quest for immortality has been through our ability to create. By painting a picture, building a building, or writing a book, we live on through our creative work. When we hear the term *immortal works of art,* we realize that at least the memory of the artist, if not some spiritual remnant of the artist, lives on through his or her creation. There is a true sense that we preserve a vestige of ourselves for future generations through our creativity.

We also seek to unite ourselves with future generations through the achievement of greatness. By accomplishing major achievements and carving a niche for ourselves in the annals of history, we feel secure in the idea that we will not pass into oblivion. Though we die, our name and accomplishment will live on in the awareness, and perhaps appreciation, of others.

However, even though we attempt to cope with our awareness of separation by leaving a legacy through children, creativity, and greatness, there remains a deep realization that we cannot escape alienation, nor grasp immortality. Perhaps this can be seen most clearly in the life of Alexander the Great.

Alexander the Great did truly conquer "the world." His Macedonian armies triumphed over the Greek city-states and then marched on to subdue the Persian Empire from Asia Minor to Egypt and even to India. Alexander was a conqueror of conquerors. Indeed his name is still equated with the word *great* more than two thousand years after his death.

Yet the one thing Alexander realized he could not subdue was the inevitability of separation through death. It is reported that when Alexander made his own funeral arrangements, he left specific instructions that he lie in state with the palms of his hands facing upward, visibly open and empty. He wanted everyone who passed by to see a vivid symbolism that though he conquered the world, he could take nothing with him in death. Ultimately even Alexander the Great had to experience separation from all that he knew and conquered.

So we see that along with Pip in *Moby Dick*, we all experience the trauma of being cast into the middle of a cosmic ocean at birth. We frantically attempt to stay afloat, hoping that someone will come along to give us something to hold on to, to rescue us, to reunite us with our crew. But our fear is that though we manage to temporarily stay afloat, our loneliness will drown the "infinite of our soul."

STAYING AFLOAT

How can we better cope with the "prison of our aloneness"? How can we protect and sustain our sanity that Pip so tragically lost? Though we cannot eradicate loneliness and a sense of separateness from our lives, we can do several things that will help us and free us to cope with our own alienation.

Relax and Accept

When I was a teenager, I loved to fish on the Flint River. Meandering through the middle of Georgia, the Flint was filled with large bass that would lurk in the shadows of enormous trees overhanging sandy banks. As we floated down the river in flat-bottomed boats, it was a delight to carefully cast a line under the hanging moss of these trees and see if the bass would bite.

Old Mr. John had been fishing the river for years. Usually he would go alone, always carrying a shotgun with his fishing tackle. On one afternoon, Mr. John created a spectacle I will never forget.

There was one particular fishing hole Mr. John always returned to. It was tucked way under the protective branches of a huge willow tree. Some of the biggest bass on the Flint River fed there, but they were notoriously hard to catch.

On this afternoon Mr. John had already snagged three lines in the willow tree. Growing irritable and impatient, he edged his boat closer and closer until the bow was under a tangle of moss and tree limbs. Lulled by the quiet flow of the river, he was nearly asleep when he heard an ominous thud in the front of the boat. Looking down, he saw that a huge black water moccasin had dropped off a tree limb and into his boat. In panic he snatched up his twelve-gauge shotgun and shot the snake—and he also blew the bottom right out of his boat. Old Mr. John looked more than a little sheepish when some of us loud-mouthed boys picked him up floating in the middle of the river a few minutes after he had abandoned ship.

I have often thought of this story when I have been tempted to panic and overreact to dangers in my life. In our overreaction we can destroy not only the danger that threatens us, but the security that protects us as well.

Captain Ahab blew the bottom out of his boat. He was so driven to eliminate the huge whale that had caused him pain that he destroyed his own life and security in the process.

Many of us become Mr. Johns and Captain Ahabs when the loneliness and alienation of life presses down heavily upon us. We take healthy coping impulses that are God-given—the desire for friendship, marriage, sex, truth, children, creativity, and greatness—and we turn them into destructive drivenness. Rather than use these means to coexist creatively with loneliness, we demand that they obliterate and eradicate our loneliness. Never content, we insist on achieving our over-expectations until our drivenness destroys us.

The first thing that we must do to cope with the loneliness and alienation of life is to accept the fact that it will always be with us. When we can relax and accept our loneliness and stop trying to absolutely extinguish it, then we have taken a giant step toward mental and spiritual health.

Create a Support System

Several days ago I was dog paddling in a swimming pool, trying to converse with a friend who was sitting on the end of a diving board. Growing tired, I looked around for some means of flotation and noticed that my sons had left several balls floating in the water. I grasped a volleyball and clasped it to me, only to realize it would not adequately support my weight. While retaining the volleyball, I reached out and retrieved two other, smaller balls. When I held all three balls together—no small feat!—I found that their combined buoyancy could hold me up. However, any one of those three balls by themselves could not keep me afloat.

So it is with those aspects of life that help us cope with our loneliness. No one coping device can keep us afloat as we struggle with our fear of the deep. For instance, friendship by itself will not sustain us. Nor will marriage, sexuality, truth, creativity, or any other of our healthy coping mechanisms when grasped by themselves. They must be engaged collectively as part of a support system.

A support system is a balanced and multifaceted network of relationships composed of your spouse, members of your family, intimate friends, casual friends, coworkers, church members, your doctor, your pastor, and all the special relationships that contribute to your life. The combination of these relationships provides the relational buoyancy to keep you afloat when you fear you will sink into the depths of loneliness.

It is important for us to understand that we'll not make it if our support system consists of only one or two relationships. Marriages grow unhealthy when the partners have only each other for relational support. We cannot possibly provide all of the interpersonal needs a spouse requires. To expect to do so is unrealistic.

Likewise, to have one or even two "best friends" and not nurture other friendships is to place all our weight on one buoyancy ball. If that one ball should slip from our grasp for any reason, we will find ourselves adrift and without support. All of this means that for emotional and spiritual wholeness we each need a balanced and comprehensive support system of strong and varied relationships.

Contribute to the Future

It is also important for each of us to expand those activities and involvements that will enable us to make some kind of a contribution to future generations.

My paternal grandmother was a simple woman. She never went to high school. She couldn't paint, compose, or write creatively. But she could make quilts. Confined to her small apartment during Colorado blizzards, she would spend many hours with needle and thread fashioning quilts from colorful material. In good weather she would sit with the women of her sewing circle, telling stories and happily collecting gossip. Grandmother made each of her seventeen grandchildren their own special quilt.

The quilt she gave me is composed of many squares. In each square is sewn the name of one of my cousins with his or her birth date. I would not trade this quilt for any amount of money.

Grandmother died several years ago at age ninety-six. But I still have her quilt. Indeed I often use it to teach my children about the scattered members of their extended family.

Through quilting, my grandmother spent many good times with her friends. But she also created warmth and comfort and memories that bonded her to many generations to come.

Quilting isn't for everyone. Some people tell stories. I write books. One friend makes furniture, another collects recipe cards. A doctor delivers a baby, a preacher preaches a sermon, a first-grade teacher helps a child to read, a coach instills a love for sports. Each in is investing something of himself or herself into the life of another generation. In this way the usefulness and meaning of our life is being extended well beyond our years upon this earth—we shall live on even when we die.

Seek Truth

It is important that we do strive to relate to that which is ultimate in life. If it is philosophical truth, we must ponder on its profundity and mystery. If it is scientific truth, we need to explore its precision and wonder. And if, for you, truth is God, it is essential to spend time in prayer and meditation, and on the study of theology and Scripture.

Perhaps Thornton Wilder expressed this need best through the character of the Stage Manager in his play *Our Town*. With the cast gathered in a cemetery, the Stage Manager says:

Now there are some things we all know, but we don't take'm out and look at'm very often. We all know that something is eternal. And it ain't houses and it ain't names, and it ain't earth, and it ain't even the stars . . . everybody knows in their bones that something is eternal, and that something has to do with human beings. All the greatest people ever lived have been telling us that for five thousand years and yet, you'd be surprised how many people are always losing hold of it. There's something way down deep that's eternal about every human being.[8] (Coward–McCann, 1938)

Yes, there are some things we all know. But we don't "take'm out and look at'm very often." And if there is ultimate and eternal truth in this universe, we are far healthier if we are not always "losing hold of it."

We have seen in our reflections that one of the strongest drives within men and women is to overcome a primal and innate sense of separation and to achieve a feeling of unity and relationship in this world. This drive toward unity takes us down many healthy and pleasant roads that lead to friendship, marriage, sexual union, a search for truth, and a desire to contribute to future generations.

But the same drive for unity can lead to destructive behavior when we refuse to accept the fact that loneliness is an inevitable part of life and cannot be totally eradicated from our experience. To refuse to accept this reality of life is to jeopardize the health of our relationships by creating over-expectations and impossible demands upon others. Though we cannot completely remove the sense of separation in each other's lives, we can share in this experience together. After all, if you've got to be a castaway, it's nice to have company on that desert island.

Conclusion

FINDING
CONTENTMENT

I HAVE ALWAYS BEEN AMAZED BY THE HUMAN BIRTH PROCESS. As I have walked with Beth through three pregnancies and the delivery of each of our children, I have developed a sense of awe at the wonder of creation and the innate sense of motherhood that develops in a woman.

I am intrigued by how a woman's body instinctively knows when to deliver a baby. For many weeks the child slowly develops in its mother's womb. And then on perfect cue, when the baby is fully formed, labor begins and a new life is brought into the world. It is amazing!

During the birth of our children I have reflected on how the natural forces of life seem to be pushing and prodding us all somewhere.

It seems to me that the drivenness of our lives, though frequently destructive, can also serve as the wrenching labor pains that squeeze us into the birth of a new and vital relationship with God. Perhaps this is what Jesus meant when he looked at the harried and quizzical face of a searching Nicodemus and said, "You must be born again" (John 3:7).

Paul, too, sensed that the elements of our lives that goad and enslave us might only be the labor pains that are leading us to the birth of a new awareness of God. In the Epistle to the Romans, as translated by J. B. Phillips, Paul writes:

> The world of creation cannot as yet see reality, not because it chooses to be blind, but because in God's purpose it has been so limited—yet it has been given hope. And the hope is that in the end the whole of created life will be rescued from the tyranny of change and decay, and have its share in that magnificent liberty which can only belong to the children of God!
>
> It is plain to anyone with eyes to see that at the present time all created life groans in a sort of universal travail [childbirth].[1] (8:20-22)

Up to now our thinking has been primarily focused on the negative aspects of our human drivenness. But I am equally convinced that the impetus of our drivenness may also positively serve as the birth contractions that push us toward God.

A vast array of personalities illustrate how our compulsive quests, though costly, can ultimately lead us to God. But I want to focus our attention on one—a man who lived more than sixteen hundred years ago, Saint Augustine of Hippo.

Augustine was born in 354 in Tagaste, Numidia, a North African town near the eastern border of present-day Algeria. His father, Patricius, was a landowner and a pagan. His mother, Monica, was a devout Christian.

As a child, Augustine received a Christian education in his home from his mother. Very early he exhibited great intellectual and academic promise. At the age of sixteen he was sent to the university city of Carthage to study rhetoric and oratory in hopes that he would become a lawyer.

During these impressionable years Augustine began to feel the undercurrents of drivenness within him. Seeking his own truth, he renounced Christianity. And feeling the passion of sexuality stirring, he began to live with a mistress. Though he never mentions her name in his writings, he lived with her for fifteen years and together they had a son, Adeodatus.

As Augustine continued to be driven to find meaning in life, he read Cicero's treatise, *Hortensius,* a document now lost to history. Under the spell of Cicero's logic, he fell in love with philosophy and abandoned his desire to be a lawyer.

Nonetheless, religious sensitivity continued to influence Augustine. He became an adherent of a now extinct sect called Manichaeanism, a very eclectic faith drawing from Christianity, gnosticism, Buddhism, and other cults. Adherents of Manichaeanism were influenced by astrology and followed strict religious practices, such as vegetarianism. Augustine remained a Manichaean for nine years.

During his twenties Augustine moved to Rome to begin a school of rhetoric. He soon became disillusioned by the lethargic attitudes of his students, and he decided to abandon teaching. Augustine was also becoming disillusioned with himself. With both his health and finances near ruin, he was becoming increasingly critical of his own moral and spiritual condition. He decided to start over and sent his mistress and son home to North Africa while he moved to Milan.

Continuing to be impelled by a desire for truth, he abandoned Manichaeanism and became swayed by a philosophy called Neoplatonism. At the same time he met the able Christian bishop of Milan, Ambrose, who also began to influence him. Over time he rediscovered the Christian faith of his mother, Monica, but on terms that were now his own. At the age of thirty-two he had a profound religious experience and was baptized as a Christian.

A man of immense talent, Augustine became a priest at age thirty-seven. When he was forty-two he was consecrated as the bishop of his native region of Hippo, North Africa. For thirty-five years he served as a pastor and a bishop and became one of the most influential theological voices within the history of the Christian church. Today he is regarded as one of the most prominent church fathers and shapers of Western thought.

Fortunately for us who currently struggle, Augustine was a warm and down-to-earth person who was open about his inner conflicts.

In one of his major works, *The Confessions,* Augustine allows his reader to gain insight into the factors that prompted him toward the Christian faith. Many of these influences are the same issues we have looked at in this book—the desire for the blessing, secrets of shame, seeking forgiveness, the discovery of grace, destructive scripts, sexuality, a keen sense of relational loneliness, and a passion for discovering ultimate truth. All of these dynamics brought Augustine to embrace Christianity.

Reflecting on his conversion experience, Augustine made two statements that have greatly influenced me. First, he said, "There is a God-shaped vacuum in every man that only Christ can fill."[2] Second, he prayerfully exclaimed to God, "Thou hast made us for Thyself, and restless are our hearts until they find rest in Thee."[3] Let us look closely at these personal confessions.

THE GOD-SHAPED VACUUM

A vacuum is caused by emptiness. When all matter has been removed from a space and a void has been produced, a force field is created that attempts to suck matter back into the vacancy.

One of the major causes of our drivenness is a spiritual emptiness within us that demands to be filled. However, a vacuum does not discriminate as to what objects its empty hunger draws inside itself. A household vacuum cleaner rolled across a floor will just as easily suck up a diamond ring as it will lint and dirt. And a human being is also prone to fill his or her spiritual emptiness with whatever is closest at hand—diamonds or dirt.

As Augustine moved along in life, his spiritual hunger caused him to try to fill his emptiness with many things—friendship, sexuality, children, teaching, ambitions, philosophy, Manichaeanism, rhetoric, and art. But there came a time when Augustine realized that the jagged, vacuous hole in his life was "God-shaped." He discovered that only God could fill his hungering emptiness.

If Augustine is correct, and I believe he is, a positive influence of drivenness can be a dawning awareness of spiritual emptiness in our lives that only God can fill. Indeed God has created us with this "hole in our heart" so that, through the course of our lives, we may have an access by which a natural drivenness attracts us to him. Like a homing pigeon returning to her roost, we have an uncanny ability to be drawn to the source of our creation, God. For this reason, Augustine exclaimed, "Thou has made us for Thyself, and restless are our hearts until they find their rest in Thee."

THE FREUDIAN REFUTATION

In 1856, almost fifteen hundred years after the birth of Augustine, Sigmund Freud was born in Austria. The worldview that encompassed Freud's life was vastly different than Augustine's. While Augustine's age was shaped by the metaphysical views of philosophy, Freud was born into the fledgling era of the Age of Science.

Like Augustine, Freud was intellectually brilliant and was deeply interested in seeking truth. Freud was particularly fascinated with the dynamics of human behavior and is considered the father of modern psychology.

Concurring with Augustine, Freud noted that there is something within the nature of people that draws them toward God. However, rather than accepting this phenomenon as evidence for the existence of God, Freud radically departed company with Augustine and stated that God is an illusion or our desire for "wish-fulfillment."

Freud argued that men and women never lose their desire for pre-birth symbiosis nor their childhood need to be protected by their father and mother. For this reason adults will psychologically project or create a being they call "God" who is a "super-parent." For Freud, this God was only an illusion, but a useful one. It provided a sense of comfort, stability, and well-being.

Freud would agree with Augustine that there is a "restlessness in our hearts" that causes us to think of God. But for him and others like him, God is only a myth.

A Decision

Augustine and Freud arrive at dramatically opposed conclusions, but they do agree on one major premise: Men and women are relentlessly driven to something they call "God." However, whether God truly exists is the question of the ages.

Like the character depicted by Robert Frost in his poem "The Road Not Taken," we find ourselves on life's journey perplexed and at a loss for spiritual direction. We come to a major fork in our road and we must decide whether we believe God exists or whether He is simply a helpful illusion. Which road of belief shall we choose to travel? We cannot travel both.

In an earlier book I suggested that we cannot empirically prove the existence of God.[4] Our intellect and reason will only bring us to a point of probability. It is at this point that we reach the fork in the road and must decide whether we will take the road of faith (Augustine) or the road of nonbelief (Freud).

Blaise Pascal, a brilliant French mathematician, physicist, and religious philosopher of the seventeenth century, faced just such a choice. As with Augustine, the drivenness in Pascal's life brought him to his fork in the road, and he was pressed to make his decision concerning the existence of God. One night while pondering his decision, he anxiously scribbled these words in a journal: "Seeing too much to doubt and too little to be sure, I am in a state to be pitied."[5] Many of us have found ourselves in such a moment of anxiety.

Another young man in the New Testament, the frantic father of a critically ill little boy, came to this same point of perplexity. When confronted with the healing power of Jesus, he exclaimed, "I believe; help my unbelief!" (Mark 9:24). With Pascal, he had seen "too much to doubt and too little to be sure." He stood in indecision and had to make a choice.

Many times in life we must make decisions without possessing enough facts or information to be absolutely sure that we are right. Indeed, we usually make minor decisions with our head and major decisions with our heart. When deciding upon marriage, vocation, and belief in God, we gauge what we do know over against what we don't know and then make an intuitive choice. We take a leap of faith influenced by reason but motivated by the impulse of our heart.

When we stand at our fork in the road, one thing is clear—we can't stay there forever. Life moves on. Lacking surety, we must choose one way or the other and continue on. The correctness of our decisions will be told in the future of our journey.

Late one night when I was fifteen years old I picked up a magazine and read about an organization called the Amigos de las Americas. This unique agency trains and sends teenagers to work as medics in underdeveloped countries during their summer vacations. The "Amigos" give inoculations, simple first aid, and teach health care and hygiene. I was captivated by the article and decided to apply to work in the program.

A year later I found myself nervously standing on an airstrip in Houston, Texas, waiting to board a charter airplane for Honduras. This young Georgia boy was a long way from home, and I felt like I was going to the end of the earth.

Looking around I saw all the other Amigos assigned to Guatemala, Honduras, and El Salvador. There were only two of us from Georgia, and I did not see anyone that I knew. I felt lonely and, though I would not admit it, I was very anxious and frightened.

In a matter of seconds I reevaluated my decision. Yes, I wanted to go to Honduras. I wanted to do something worthwhile with my life. And I felt that maybe this experience would help me decide whether I really wanted to be a doctor.

Yet what if I was dumped way out in the middle of nowhere and was miserable? What if I wanted to come home? What if I got sick? I began to feel like a frantic child spending the night away from home for the first time.

Standing on that airstrip with suitcase held in sweating hand, there was no way to see into the future. I had to make the trip to know the outcome, and a decision could not be postponed. With unsure steps I walked toward the plane.

As I suspected, it was a tough summer. I did miss home. And I did get sick. But the experience changed my life. In the process of working in the midst of extreme poverty and preventable disease, I became convinced that God was real and that he had a purpose for my life. And very simply, that purpose was to help other people and to be a part of reducing suffering in this world.

I might never have gained this insight if I hadn't made the trip. I never could have made my discovery from reading an article safely removed from the actual experience of poverty and suffering and pain. I had to make a decision to board a plane and risk the journey.

The same is true in our search for God. We cannot read about God or think about God and find adequate basis to believe in God. It is only when we come to our fork in the road—our decision to board the plane—and decide to commit ourselves to the journey of faith that we come to see that God is real.

In such moments of deciding between belief and disbelief, we must remember that when Jesus invited his friends to be his disciples, he did not say to them, "Believe in me." He did not debate with them, distribute gospel tracts, or talk about philosophy and doctrine. He simply said, "Follow me." Jesus knew that deep spiritual belief can only be spawned over a long process of time and the experiences of a lifetime. Whether or not a road proves to be the correct one can only be discovered when we faithfully follow its length and discover its destination.

In traveling life's road, I cautiously took the road of Augustine, of Pascal, of the frantic father, and of Jesus. I decided to believe in God. Admittedly, there have been a few days when I have wondered if I'd made a mistake. But there have been far more days when I have known with conviction that my choice was the right one.

As I'm sure it has been with you, I've spent much time and energy trying to get others to give me the illusive blessing. I have repressed secrets, sought forgiveness, and hungered for grace. Hiding behind an outgoing personality and friendly smile, I have agonized in my loneliness and isolation. I have felt the breath of death upon my neck and have run away. Yet somehow this restlessness and drivenness has brought me to increasing certainty of the existence of God.

Ultimately, I have come to be thankful even for the drivenness within me. Though it has sometimes caused me to sail empty seas and engage in futile pursuits, it has also drawn me to faith in God. I have discovered that without hunger I can never be filled, that without thirst I can never drink deeply of the joy of life, and without wrestling with drivenness I can never be drawn to God.

Hunger, thirst, and drivenness can kill us. But these very same forces of potential destruction are also the elements that make life so very rich and worth living. I am thankful that there is a gaping hole in my heart that can only be filled by God. And I am content to be restless until I "find my rest in thee."

NOTES

Introduction: How Can We Stop Being Driven?

1. Samuel Taylor Coleridge, "The Rime of the Ancient Mariner," *Lyrical Ballads* (1798). As quoted by Bergen Evans in *Dictionary of Quotations* (New York: Bonanza Books, 1968), 739.

2. Eugene Ehrlich, Stuart Berg Flexner, Gorton Carruth, and Joyce M. Hawkins, compilers, *Oxford American Dictionary* (New York: Oxford University Press, 1980), 196.

3. Herman Melville, *Moby Dick, or, The Whale* (Norwalk, Conn.: The Easton Press, 1977), 582.

One: Accept the Blessing

1. Jesus Sirach 3:11. Gerhard Kittel, ed., *Theological Dictionary of the New Testament* Vol. II (Grand Rapids, Mich.: Eerdmans, 1964), 754ff.

2. Though the psychological term *the blessing* is frequently used in theological circles and can be attributed to no specific person, I am indebted to Dr. Myron C. Madden for his writing and popularization of this concept. Particularly helpful are his books *The Power to Bless* (Nashville: Abingdon Press, 1970); *Claim Your Heritage* (Philadelphia: The Westminster Press, 1984); and *Blessing: Giving the Gift of Power* (Nashville: Broadman Press, 1988).

3. Will Dunham. "As U.S. Marriage Rate Falls, Experts Fret." AOL News, America Online, Sept. 21, 1999.

4. George Gallup Jr., and George O'Connell, *Who Do Americans Say That I Am?* (Philadelphia: Westminster Press, 1986), 88.

5. James Arthur Baldwin, (1924–87), source unknown.

6. Judith Viorst, *Necessary Losses* (New York: Simon and Schuster, 1986), 230.

7. Ibid., 234.

8. Howard M. Halpern, *Cutting Loose: A Guide to Adult Terms with Your Parents* (New York: Bantam Books, 1977), 126.

9. John Powell, an address given at Furman University, July 1978.

10. Daniel J. Levinson, et al., *The Seasons of a Man's Life* (New York: Alfred A. Knopf, 1978), 97–99.

11. Paul Tournier, *A Place for You* (New York: Harper & Row, 1969), 180.

12. Joachim Jeremias, *The Prayers of Jesus* (London: SCM Press, 1967), 29, 53, 57.

Two: Let Go of Secrets and Shame

1. Paul Tournier, *Secrets* (Richmond, Va.: John Knox Press, 1965), 8.

2. Ibid., 18–19.

3. "Psychologists Finally Focus on the Master Emotion," *The Charleston News and Courier* (October 5, 1987): 10-B.

4. Ibid.

5. Ibid.

6. Pat Conroy, *The Prince of Tides* (Boston: Houghton Mifflin, 1986), 82.

7. Scott Walker, *Where the Rivers Flow* (Waco, Tex.: Word Books, 1986).

Three: Receive Forgiveness and Grace

1. On the subject of masturbation and guilt, see Karl Menninger, *Whatever Became of Sin* (New York: Hawthorne Books, 1973), 31–37.

2. Saint Augustine, *Confessions,* Book II, chapter 14.

Four: Confront Deadly Scripts

1. Eric Berne in one of the major theoretical contributors to the concept of Script Analysis. For more information see Eric Berne, *Transactional Analysis in Psychotherapy* (New York: Grove Press, 1961).

2. Meyer Friedman, and Ray H. Rosenman, *Type A Behavior and Your Heart* (Greenwich, Conn.: Fawcett Publications, 1974).

3. Rev. Steven Shoemaker, Meyers Baptist Church, Charlotte, S.C.

4. William Shakespeare, *As You Like It* (II, 7).

Five: Overthrow the Tyranny of Possessions

1. Mark Twain, *The Tragedy of Pudd'nhead Wilson,* heading of chapter 2 (1894).

2. Harold Kushner, *When All You've Ever Wanted Isn't Enough* (New York: Simon and Schuster, 1986), 82.

3. Abraham Maslow, *Motivation and Personality* (New York: Harper & Row, 1970).

4. Henry James, *The Portrait of a Lady* (Norwalk, Conn.: The Easton Press, 1978), 6.

5. Elisabeth Elliot. *Christian Herald* (January 15, 1985): 5.

6. George Herbert, *Herald of Holiness* (November 15, 1985): 5.

7. Forrest Carter, *The Education of Little Tree* (Albuquerque, N. Mex.: University of New Mexico Press, 1976), 6–11.

8. Erich Fromm, *The Art of Loving* (New York: Harper & Row, 1956), 24.

Six: Connect with Others

1. Herman Melville, *Moby Dick, or, The Whale* (Norwalk, Conn.: The Easton Press, 1977). 443.

2. Ibid.

3. Erich Fromm. *The Art of Loving* (New York: Harper & Row, 1956), 8–9.

4. Francis Bacon, *De Dignitate et Augmentis Scientiarum* (1640), 37.

5. Jean-Paul Sartre, *Huis Clos,* sc. V.

6. Judith Viorst, *Necessary Losses* (New York: Simon and Schuster, 1986), 170–171.

7. Scott Walker, *Liferails: Holding Fast to God's Promises* (Minneapolis: Augsburg Fortress, 1999), 40–41.

8. Thornton Wilder, *Our Town* (New York: Bantam Books, 1966 [Coward-McCann, 1938]), 52.

Conclusion: Finding Contentment

1. J. B. Phillips, Romans 8:20-22, *The New Testament in Modern English* (New York: Macmillan, 1958, 1959, 1960), 324.

2. Saint Augustine, *Inspiring Quotations,* edited by Albert M. Wells Jr. (Nashville: Thomas Nelson Publishers, 1988), 121.

3. Saint Augustine, *Confessions,* Book I.

4. Scott Walker, *Where the Rivers Flow: Exploring the Sources of Faith Development* (Waco, Texas: Word Books, 1986).

5. Blaise Pascal as quoted by Daniel Taylor, in *The Myth of Certainty* (Waco, Tex.: Word Books, 1986), 65.